3/4
50

NATIONAL CHARACTER IN ACTION

NATIONAL CHARACTER IN ACTION — *Intelligence Factors in Foreign Relations*

BY

WASHINGTON PLATT
Brigadier General USAR—Ret.

RUTGERS UNIVERSITY PRESS
New Brunswick   *New Jersey*

CB 197
P6

DEDICATION

To all those concerned with
Foreign Intelligence and Foreign Relations
who are striving to do a little better

YET SOM THERE BE . . .
TO SUCH MY ERRAND IS. . . .

John Milton: *Comus*

PREFACE

Nations differ in their national character as much as individuals differ in personal character. For success in international relations it is just as profitable, and indeed just as essential, to understand the character of the nation with which one is dealing as it is to understand the character of an individual in personal dealings. This maxim applies equally to friends, neutrals, and potential enemies.

In all aspects of international relations and especially in the formulation and implementation of foreign policy, an intimate understanding of the character of other nations must always be one of the vital factors in the situation—usually one of the first factors. Such understanding becomes part of almost every phase of foreign policy planning and execution. It is an essential element of any international problems, whether the genesis of the problem be military, diplomatic, economic, political, psychological or cultural.

National character includes the predominant traits in the character of individuals within a nation, the effective character of influential groups, and finally the coalescence of individual and group desires when a people responds to a crisis *as a nation*. The term national character has been chosen for the title of this book because it is widely used

vii

and generally understood. Its exact meaning is developed in the first few sections of the text and in Appendix A.

"The spirit of the people" has a somewhat similar meaning, but is broader than "national character." The spirit of the people expresses quite clearly the less technical aspect of this subject. It is the human aspect free from the weight of scientific jargon. In other words: *What kind of people are they?* This is a case where no single term brings out the full meaning of the concept.

Purpose

There is a growing interest in foreign affairs shown by the citizens of the United States, and by many parts of the United States government. At the same time there is a healthy and much needed critical scrutiny of our Foreign Service and of our Foreign Intelligence and a demand that we should leave no stone unturned to bring both of these up to the highest possible level. The present book is intended as a small contribution to this great cause.

The purpose of the present study is to invite attention to the importance of national character as a vital element in international relations and foreign intelligence, to describe its nature, capabilities and limitations; and to show its role in understanding foreign peoples, in formulating foreign policy, and its applications to intelligence production in support of such policy.

To be perfectly clear, I claim:

1. An understanding of national character is one of the basic factors in good foreign intelligence.
2. Good foreign intelligence is essential to good international relations and to our national security in peace and in war.

3. Our Intelligence Community and our Foreign Service have unnecessarily and dangerously neglected this basic factor.

It has been well said that our Foreign Service is the first line of defense in our organization for national security. History shows us all too clearly that wars take up only when diplomacy leaves off.

The initial responsibility falls upon our Foreign Service. The effectiveness of the calculated risk in negotiation depends upon knowledge, for in diplomacy, as in every field of endeavor, knowledge is strength. And this knowledge comes from foreign intelligence in the broadest sense of the word, including of course reports from our embassies abroad.

Reliable foreign intelligence is *the firm foundation* upon which can be built diplomatic offense or defense. There is no more vital element in the complex structure of our international relations and our national defense. If foreign intelligence is utilized by first-class men using the best methods, it is a source of great strength. If neglected, then the United States is put in the position of a blind man starting out to fight a duel.

Practical Application—A Pioneering Effort

I hope that this book will supply a convenient summary of some of the excellent work on national character which has already been done. However, its elements of originality and the justification for its publication in this form lie in its emphasis on the *practical applications of the concept of national character to problems of foreign intelligence and to foreign relations*. To be most helpful, such practical applications must include not only basic principles and methods, with examples, but also an explanation of the special fields of usefulness of such applications, their limitations, and the opportunities for their further study.

As far as I can learn this is the first systematic attempt which has ever been made to bring together from many directions what is known about the concept of national character; and then to *apply* this concept to the problems of foreign intelligence and foreign relations with the specific object of getting out of national character every aspect of practical usefulness that there is in it.

To understand the applications of national character to foreign relations one must evidently understand something of political mechanisms and foreign relations—and of foreign intelligence, which is a fundamental part thereof. This need is the reason for my inclusion of the descriptions of some of the key factors which govern the operations of groups and nations, or which may be necessary to consider in an intelligence estimate.

The modern world is a world of change. Constant emphasis is therefore here placed upon factors which may lead to changes in the national character and in the political conditions which may have perhaps existed for centuries. Indications which can give warnings of an approaching change are pointed out.

The present discussion constitutes a new field of applied political science. It is based upon my ten years or more of practical experience with this activity in peace and in war.

The present book is one of a trilogy in the field of foreign intelligence and international relations.[1]

In this new field which deals with practical applications, I agree with Potter (20) that it is better to "speak the language of the [common] people," rather than to attempt to use the highly theoretical terms of the anthropologist, the psychologist, or, worse still, of the psychoanalyst.

Fields of Usefulness

I have attempted to write a book which will be useful to the following classes of people in the ways described:

First, *those who would like to extend their general knowledge of national character.*

Such people may be concerned with international relations at various levels. They include: the educated general public and leaders of public opinion; members of the United States Foreign Service; members of the United States Intelligence Community; other members of the United States government, whether executive or legislative, having to do with foreign affairs; businessmen concerned with international trade; those studying international affairs at the universities; and finally social scientists and others working in related disciplines, such as social psychology, cultural anthropology, history, and philosophy.

Second, *those who have definite responsibilities to take some form of action in this field.*

Such action may include responsibility to produce intelligence estimates, or to formulate and to execute foreign policy, to make plans for national defense, to conduct international negotiations, or to disseminate information about the United States. This second group may need to go a bit deeper than the first group and may find here some material and some guidance which will help each of them to look up the character of the foreign nation concerned and to determine which traits of character will be significant to the problem at hand.

Finally, *those who must conduct for themselves research in depth into the character of the people concerned, or who are directly responsible for the conduct of such research when carried out by others and for its practical applications.*

Such persons are usually faced with some new problem in foreign intelligence or foreign relations, where great issues are at stake and where national character is a critical factor. In foreign relations the usual field studies are seldom possible, so other methods must be used as are here described.

Limitations

To avoid misunderstanding and possible disappointment, I should point out that this book may be considered to contain a *set of tools with suggestions for their use* in problems of foreign intelligence production and foreign relations. For this important purpose I offer in the Supplement critical bibliography of the best current publications which describe the national character of each of many specific nations.

The book does *not* attempt to do the work of the intelligence officer or foreign service officer for him. It does not contain a table in which the answers can be found, as in a table of compound interest.

Each event in which foreign intelligence or foreign affairs would be concerned is to a considerable extent a unique event; therefore the judgment of the worker must still be called upon to decide the kind of tool and the manner of its application in each situation. So in offering the concept of national character as a tool, an author can present much that is helpful in methods, capabilities, limitations, examples and references for more extended study. Beyond this, into the solution of individual problems, I do not pretend to go. Here the reader must pick up the ball for himself; or, to be consistent with the metaphor, he must pick up the proper tool and get to work with it.

It is evident also that in treating a subject as broad as national character, which touches on all of the social and behavioral sciences, and the principles of intelligence production, this book can be no more than an introduction. For further acquaintance—I hope for further pleasant and profitable acquaintance—a good start is provided by the references in the Bibliography.

If the present book can stimulate interest in this vital subject, and can open some doors to further study, it will thereby make its own small contribution toward international understanding and to national security.

Acknowledgments

In the preparation of this book I am deeply indebted to many—many more than can be mentioned here individually.

Among those who gave freely of their time and wisdom in personal conferences on various aspects of this book are: Professors David Riesman and George Kirk of Harvard; Professors F. S. C. Northrop, K. W. Deutsch, D. M. Potter and W. R. Emerson of Yale; Professor Otto Klineberg of Columbia; Mr. Warren C. House of Washington, D.C.; and Mr. Geoffrey Gorer of England.

No one but myself is responsible for the final wording, statements or conclusions.

Grateful acknowledgment is extended to the following for kind permission to quote from their publications, as is indicated in each case by references to the Bibliography of this book: Doubleday & Company, Inc., Alfred A. Knopf, Inc., W. W. Norton & Company, Inc., The Macmillan Company, Atlantic Monthly Press, John Wiley & Sons, Inc., and Technology Press of Massachusetts Institute of Technology, Social Science Research Council, Harvard University Press, Yale University Press, Stanford University Press, University of Chicago Press.

Thanks are due to the *Military Review*, published by the United States Army Command and General Staff College, for permission to use parts of my article on national character which appeared in the August, 1959, issue.
Baltimore, Maryland

The research and writing of this book were made possible by a fellowship for "studies of the basic principles of strategic intelligence in relation to national security" granted to me by the John Simon Guggenheim Memorial Foundation. I am deeply grateful to this foundation for its assistance; and also to Dr. Henry Allen Moe, the Secretary General, for his good advice, patience and kindly encouragement.

W. P.

Baltimore, Maryland
March 3, 1961

CONTENTS

NATIONAL CHARACTER IN ACTION

INTRODUCTION

Until World War I the United States was the most isolated of all the great powers—physically, mentally and politically. Within thirty years the United States became the leading power in the movement for world co-operation. Now we find ourselves the strongest power in the world economically, militarily and politically. Neutral nations as well as our allies look to us for leadership in a field in which we have heretofore had comparatively little interest or experience. Hence foreign relations present the most difficult and the most important of all the problems facing this country.

At the same moment, international relations assume an overwhelming and vitally urgent importance due to the cold war, guided missiles and the possibilities of a nuclear war. At the same moment also, the poker game of international relations begins to be played with a more deadly earnestness and an increased sophistication by all the players.

How can amateurs such as we are maintain ourselves in this cutthroat game against experienced professionals? How can we provide the leadership which the world needs and which only the United States can supply at this time?

These sudden demands upon us have aroused an active response. In typical American fashion we have shown ourselves willing to plunge in and do something about it. Politically the United States is no longer isolationist. There has been an outburst of public interest in foreign affairs. Organizations for the discussion of international relations have spread. Foreign affairs are outstandingly well-reported in our better newspapers. Scholarly journals and books on international subjects have multiplied. All of this is in the right direction. However, much of it is amateurish. Some branches of the United States government are still far below the high standards required for today's competition. In short, our reaction has been commendable, but our achievements to date are far from adequate.

There is a great need for more of the professional touch—for more professional experience and thoroughness. Just as professional engineers, and not amateurs, are employed for large engineering projects, so professional economists, area specialists, intelligence officers with professional competence, and others in their fields should have more voice in the foreign service and in foreign intelligence production.[1]

We are still extraordinarily weak, too, in our advanced training for foreign service and foreign intelligence production. Compare the thorough and systematic training in military techniques, tactics, and strategy and the graduate courses at any good university on topics connected with foreign relations with the brief or mediocre courses given in intelligence production anywhere within the United States government. We are suffering also from a failure to do the basic research in intelligence production and in some aspects of international relations from which springs an understanding of basic principles. A study of principles leads in turn to better methods. We are still woefully weak in our real understanding of many foreign peoples.[2]

As one example, our failure to understand national character was strikingly evident in the case of the Castro revolution in Cuba. Equally evident was our failure to accept the fact that revolutionists in Cuba must necessarily be quite different from revolutionists in the United States. We failed also to understand the personal characters of Castro and the other leading revolutionaries, and to make the best of the situations which presented themselves at various stages.

This weakness in our foreign intelligence is nothing new. In 1946 Pettee (7A) said: "Within our own hemisphere our government has misjudged almost every revolution for thirty years."

A study of national character starts with a realization that the character of other peoples is usually very different from our own. It is useless to *pretend* they are like ourselves, and it is foolish to try to change them to conform to our patterns. The interests of the United States are best served in the long run by taking these assumptions as starting points.

Our handling of these events is another illustration of the need for *National Character in Action* and for a better use of this intelligence factor in our foreign relations (to paraphrase the title of this book).

How Broad Is the Field?

International relations may cover any subject which affects the interests of the United States in its dealing with foreign countries. This means that there is hardly any subject in heaven or earth which may not at some time come under consideration.

The coverage is *global*, because any part of the globe

may be considered. It is, in fact, beginning to be *inter-global*. Missiles and orbiting bodies in outer space are already subjects for international agreements.

The coverage is *interdisciplinary* (a word so fashionable in academic circles). Any or all of the so-called disciplines, such as economics, sociology, military science, political science, religion, may be included. As to the United States government the coverage may be also *interdepartmental,* touching as it does on the Department of State, Departments of Defense, Army, Navy and Air Force, Central Intelligence Agency, and often having special problems which may concern the United States Department of Agriculture, Department of Commerce, the Treasury, United States Information Agency and others.

The origin of an international problem may extend backward in *time* to the Roman Empire, or even back to the Hebrew prophets. It may, and often must, look forward for twenty-five years or as much farther as we dare to peer into the *Fog of the Future.*

This wide coverage of the problems of international relations or of foreign intelligence production in space, time, disciplines, and departments presents one of the great difficulties for work in this field. There is always the temptation and the danger of spreading one's efforts too thin. Some problems are so interdisciplinary that they require a team of several experts rather than one man for their solution. So in this field, it is always desirable to attempt to limit each problem to manageable proportions, to define it as clearly as possible, and to concentrate on the fundamentals. National character is one of these fundamentals which can shed light upon many aspects of an international problem.

In such a broad field—international, interdisciplinary, interdepartmental, and with no fixed boundaries of time

—it is natural to find little in the way of a common background among the workers, little common doctrine, or even common vocabulary. Furthermore, intelligence production is an immature, that is, it is *an undisciplined discipline*. We cannot be surprised if different workers use the same term with different meanings.[3] For that reason it is important for a writer to make clear, first to himself and then to his readers, what he means by the terms that he uses.

The Central Problem

In any foreign problem we should certainly learn everything that history, geography, economics, sociology, and other matters of fact and statistics can teach us. But we want to go beyond the statistics. We want to know what kind of people these really are that make up the foreign nation with which we are concerned. Such a description starts where the statistics leave off. Beyond the statistics and the hard facts, what are the people like who must man their own institutions, exploit their own natural resources, fire their own weapons, and solve their own problems?

The moral of this book is simple, namely: *In every problem of international relations, the character of the people concerned must always be considered.* Time spent on learning and describing this factor is time well spent. Neglect leaves dangerous blind spots.

All our considerations of personal or international relations will include, whether we like it or not, some formal or informal concept or mental picture of the person or nation with which we are dealing. This picture may be built upon extensive knowledge, or it may be built upon assumptions and prejudices. If we do not have well-founded knowledge, we will then use unfounded assumptions. No one can deal physically or mentally with a blank image.

Professional Judgment

In solving problems where human reactions are involved, such as in international relations or in foreign intelligence production, it will seldom be possible to find a worthwhile answer in any table, or to get a final answer from any sort of an equation or computer. For the best answers to such problems we must always ultimately rely upon the judgment of a well-informed man of experience, proven competence, and wisdom. With the benefit of his experience and training, such a man selects, interprets and puts together the *facts* of many kinds to gain *understanding*. He then uses his understanding, supported by study, discussion, and mature thoughts to provide the sound judgment required for the solution of the problem. Some of the more general problems connected with the interpretation of data and the means for developing judgment in a given field will be discussed in detail in my third book on *Guidance from Uncertain Evidence* (8).

Research can provide many tools and much material to assist the professional foreign service officer or intelligence officer in reaching a wise decision. Needed improvements in training and professional development can do much to provide men who are better qualified professionally. We cannot hope for first-rate results from any but first-rate men. We see no means in sight for finding any substitute for expert professional judgment.

In their dependence upon the professional judgment of men having experience and understanding rather than upon fixed formulas—decisions pertaining to national character and foreign relations are in exactly the same position as decisions on personal character, business, military tactics, politics, and nearly all problems involving human relations.

However, professional competence confers great advantages: in forming judgments in any of these fields, systematic study saves time and makes for clear thinking; a knowledge of fundamental principles gives meaning to isolated facts; case histories and analogies may guide our steps. Reading the experiences and opinions of others in situations related to our own problem greatly extends the knowledge which can be gained from our unaided personal experience. Critical thought helps us to avoid pitfalls.

So although decisions on national character must ultimately depend upon subjective judgment, yet judgment in this field can be tremendously improved and the danger of serious errors greatly decreased by a consideration of the basic principles—such as those here presented—and followed by further study as here indicated.

The use of the concept of national character involves rewards and pitfalls. The only sure way to avoid pitfalls is never to attempt anything. A military man will never fail in an attack if he never attacks. In spite of some built-in uncertainties, a consideration of the character of the people is inseparable from a well-balanced assessment of any given present situation and probable future developments in foreign countries.

The Real Meaning of Foreign Intelligence[4]

Strategic intelligence is all intelligence of foreign countries other than combat intelligence. In this book "foreign intelligence" is often used interchangeably with "strategic intelligence."

Strategic or foreign intelligence is the systematic,

broad, long-range intelligence of all important aspects of each foreign country which may well affect the national interests of the United States in peace and in war. Good intelligence of a foreign country provides that insight which leads to UNDERSTANDING.

The ultimate objective of foreign intelligence is a *sympathetic understanding* of each foreign country—knowledge of the present and near-future national policies, capabilities, vulnerabilities, aspirations, and probable courses of action under given circumstances of friends, neutrals and potential enemies.[5]

Foreign Intelligence and the Foreign Service

For countless years diplomatic representatives have reported political and biographical intelligence of the countries to which they were accredited. Our foreign representatives, including consuls, now regularly report economic, agricultural, scientific, military, naval and other intelligence in a perfectly open and well-understood manner. Such information flows openly, as it should, between the nations. Human relations between friends and others are most pleasant and profitable when all parties understand each other.

In spite of this, the word "intelligence" is sometimes misunderstood. This misunderstanding is fairly widespread and has done much harm. Some diplomatic representatives will say that they have nothing to do with foreign intelligence.

This point of view is due to the fact that some intelligence has a hostile intent. Some—actually a minor part—may be secret and so may be collected by clandestine methods. This is the so-called cloak-and-dagger element, associated with sensational stories of spies and undercover agents. This type of intelligence has stolen the spotlight.

Its importance is often exaggerated. However, it represents the popular idea of intelligence.

So in view of the fact that it is, and always has been, one of the primary missions of our diplomatic representatives to send to Washington a great mass of political, economic, sociological, and other intelligence, it is perfectly proper and correct to refer to the United States Foreign Service and to all of our foreign representatives as part of the Intelligence Community. It is correct to say that we rely largely upon our foreign representatives to supply much of the material from which we can form a true picture of the national character of each foreign nation. We hope that representatives of foreign countries who are accredited to the United States are conveying to their own countries true pictures of our own national character. All of this makes for sound and profitable international relations and prevents misunderstandings.

NATIONAL CHARACTER—A
PRELIMINARY STATEMENT

The importance of a serious consideration of national character in intelligence estimates and international relations arises partly from the fact that national character is an invisible but vital factor in nearly all of the principal aspects of national life, such as economic, political, military.

The second reason for the importance of a study of national character is that it can and often does give us information which cannot be obtained in any other manner.

In the production of strategic intelligence it is, of course, helpful to be as complete as possible in all factual components, such as population, exports and military strength. However, it is a grave mistake to overlook that great intangible summed up as national character and variously called "national characteristics," "national psychology," the "national mind," or the "spirit of the people." Walt Rostow (9 and 9A) has used "national style" in a related sense. A more complete title which avoids some

12

possible misunderstandings is "national characteristic patterns of behavior."

Meaning of "Character"

In considering the meaning of the word "character" and its significance, we shall start with the more familiar "personal character" and then discuss how far the concepts of personal character can be usefully extended to groups or nations.

Character is an inner quality. This inner quality often results in behavior that we can observe and perhaps measure. Thus, generosity (as a trait of character) acting on funds available (as a tangible) may result in overt behavior, such as a gift to a local charity. A generous man of moderate means may give more than a stingy man of great wealth. Character is closely related to one's underlying motives, which are not always observable as such. Motives must often be inferred from behavior. Technically speaking, character is one of the determinants of behavior. See Lindzey (10).

Character is more than a mere habit; it is something deep-rooted and long-lasting. The acts which exhibit traits of character may be the result of a conscious decision or sometimes of an unconscious decision. Often there is a moral aspect to the choice, and there may be an emotional element.[1]

These concepts of personal character can be extended by analogy, with some reservations, to groups and nations, as will be discussed later.

The Two Meanings of "National Character"

The words "national character" may have either of two quite different meanings. Both are important to those concerned with foreign intelligence and international relations. We should understand clearly which one we are talking about at any given instance. See Ginzberg (11) and Riesman (12).

Thus when talking about the "German national character," we may mean those traits of character which are predominant in a large number of German *individuals*— such traits, for example, as industry, orderliness, willingness to submit to discipline. On the other hand, we may refer to the character exhibited by Germany *as a nation* when dealing with other nations. For example, shortly before World War I, Germany as a nation exhibited traits of character associated with "rattling the sabre," such as arrogance, aggressiveness, pugnacity. It is well known, as Klineberg (13) points out, that the aggressive tendencies of a nation are not always identical with the aggressive tendencies of individuals within it.

The character of the nation, as a nation, is of course related to the character of the individuals within the nation, but is not always the same. An excellent example of the difference is the U.S.S.R. from 1945 to 1959. The U.S.S.R., as a nation, was overbearing, truculent and aggressively communistic. The great majority of the individuals in the U.S.S.R.—certainly in what was formerly European Russia—were friendly, peace-loving and not active members of the Communist party. See Stevenson (14) and United States Advisory Commission on Information (15). In 1940, Italy, as a nation under the leadership of Mussolini, demonstrated a pugnacious character, whereas most Italians, even those in uniform, were far from warlike.

So in each part of this book I shall try to make clear which of these two aspects of national character I am discussing. I shall show this by using such contrasting phrases as the following:

"The character of individuals" or "the character of
   a nation as such,"
"The character of Frenchmen" or "the character of
   France,"
"The character shown by an individual when dealing
   with others" or "the character shown by a nation
   when dealing with other nations."

Riesman (12) supports this view that it is proper to
refer to the character of a group or nation as such. He
says:

"Social character" is that part of "character" which is
shared among significant social groups and which, as most
contemporary social scientists define it, is the product of the
experience of these groups. The notion of social character
permits us to speak of the character of classes, groups,
regions, and nations.

I do not plan to argue over the many ambiguities of the
concept of social character. . . . The assumption that a social
character exists has always been a more or less invisible
premise of the social sciences.

In matters of national security the United States usually
makes its official contacts first with other nations as such.
It is the nation which makes war, makes treaties, accepts
foreign aid, or encroaches on our allies. So we are
naturally interested in the character of a given nation as
such in its dealings with us or with other nations.[2]
But we are also vitally interested in the predominant
traits of character of the individuals within each nation.
First, because the character of individuals within a nation
is an important ingredient of the character of the nation
acting officially. Second, because the predominant traits
of character of the individuals in a given nation are the

best indications of what to expect from that nation in many situations. The intelligence and foreign service officer must consider both aspects of national character.

National character is a rich concept. The more we study it the more aspects and applications we find. Like many manifestations of human activities, it must be approached from many angles in order to be well understood and used with confidence.

The Most Rewarding Approaches to Our Subject

In the case of personal character and also of national character, the psychologists, anthropologists and other scientists are making progress, but have so far failed to provide more than a small part of the knowledge necessary for making practical use of these concepts (See Appendix D). This need not deter us. For practical purposes we use the methods herein described based upon experience in addition to an elementary background of knowledge of the sciences above mentioned.

If this study were concerned with the principles of anthropology or with psychological theory instead of with the practical problems of intelligence and foreign relations, it would be worthwhile to attempt to dig more deeply into definitions of technical terms used in these fields and into the current theories. In view of the present immaturity of these sciences and the tentative nature of many of the conclusions in their fields, no benefit would result which would be useful in accomplishing the simple purposes of the present book.

Consider for a moment those who are interested in national character in order to do their own jobs more effectively. Such persons include the intelligence officer or the foreign service officer or the government official concerned with planning or policy in international relations.

Each of these men has his hands full doing his own job well. He should know how to gain and use a knowledge of national character in any one of the problems which are a part of his duties. He is on the firing line to *apply* what is known. To do this he does not have to become a professional anthropologist or psychologist.

In this connection the situation of the active intelligence officer, foreign service officer or other official, is closely similar to the position of an artillery officer in command of a battery in action against the enemy. His duties are to direct the fire of his battery against the enemy in accordance with the mission given him. Now the firing of an artillery shell is the result of many complicated chemical reactions taking place in the explosives used. Somebody must understand these reactions. However, a combat artilleryman would use his time poorly to stray into the chemical field while on a combat mission. He would do much better to take the artillery shell delivered to him and then to devote all of his professional skill to the application of these shells to the destruction of the enemy. Other men under other circumstances must of course conduct research into the chemistry and engineering pertaining to artillery weapons and ammunition.

So I feel that one of the greatest opportunities for improvement in activities pertaining to international relations is to encourage and assist those on the firing line to *apply* to foreign intelligence and foreign relations some of the useful concepts which are already available. One of these concepts capable of much more effective application than is customary at present is national character. In this book I am attempting to help the busy worker in making such applications. As a secondary consideration I point the way to broader theoretical knowledge for those who have the time to pursue it; but I make no further apology for the fact that this is a pioneering attempt to point out *applications,* and is not a contribution to scientific theory.

It is commonplace that in most of the arts, highly successful applications were known far in advance of theory. For example, thousands of useful buildings, bridges and other structures were built of wood and stone long before the science of structural engineering was developed. So we who are active in this field hope to advance the art of producing intelligence estimates and conducting foreign relations long before there is an adequate scientific explanation for our methods.

PERSONAL CHARACTER

First the Common-Sense View

Much work has been done on the study of personal character by psychologists, anthropologists and others. Yet as we shall see, from the scientific point of view the picture is far from clear. Differences of opinion exist even as to definitions of temperament, personality and character. In spite of these scientific shortcomings personal character has a very practical meaning to the ordinary man. He makes very real use of such terms as honesty, industry, bravery, loyalty, and their opposites in his dealings with his fellow men.

Therefore it seems definitely worthwhile to start with a consideration of personal character from the point of view of common sense and daily experiences, entirely apart from any scientific theories. Then we shall consider how much that is pertinent to this study can be added by psychology, anthropology, sociology, *et al.*

A sound knowledge of personal character is, of course, a necessary foundation for any study of national character.

Personal Character

Every person is a mixture of conflicting motives and traits of character. He has elements of industry and of laziness, of bravery and of fear, of generosity and of selfishness. In spite of these opposite tendencies, one person may usually act industriously, bravely and generously. This is a matter of observation, completely independent of any philosophical or psychological explanations that we may attempt to apply. Furthermore, the pattern of behavior of many people is so consistent that we can use this knowledge very profitably in our dealings with them. We should be very foolish if we did not.

As a useful working definition of "character" we quote Riesman (12): "Character, in this sense, is the more or less permanent socially and historically conditioned organization of an individual's drives and satisfactions— the kind of 'set' with which he approaches the world and people."

The character of an individual, like many other qualities of living organisms, is a product of the interaction of heredity and environment. (Environment is not here limited to physical environment; it includes culture.)

Among the bases of personal character, inborn characteristics are certainly important. For the practical purposes of this book I quote the following statement by Kluckhohn and Murray (21, p. 56):

The old problem of "heredity or environment" is essentially meaningless. The two sets of determinants can rarely be completely disentangled once the environment has begun to operate. All geneticists are agreed today that traits are not inherited in any simple sense. The observed characters of organisms are, at any given point of time, the product of a long series of complex interactions between biologically-inherited potentialities and environmental forces. The outcome of each interaction is a modification of the personality.

Starting with the little understood inborn qualities which are the bases of character, the character of an individual *is developed* over a long period by his environment. Environmental influences acting on the inborn qualities produce traits of character which are nearly always evidenced in part by overt action. Character is usually one of several determinants which influence a given action by an individual in a given situation.

What I have in mind are such traits of character as:

Industry	Will to Win
Thoroughness	Optimism
Reliability	Initiative
Generosity	Aggressiveness
Patriotism	Truthfulness
Courage	Brilliance
Tenacity	Visionary Qualities
Warlike Qualities	Spirituality
Spirit of Fair Play	Spirit of Co-operation

and their OPPOSITES

It will be noticed that each of these traits of character is more than the inborn capability to do something. All involve *a decision on the part of the individual to perform more or less of the activity in question than he has to perform in order to keep himself out of serious trouble.*[1] Thus a man may be physically strong and capable of prolonged physical exertion. This man may be industrious and work hard at digging a ditch, even when he is not watched; or he may be lazy and do just enough to hold his job. The strength is largely inborn, the industrious trait is character.

From another point of view every individual has within himself elements of industry and elements of laziness.[2] A man with an industrious character requires relatively little motivation to cause him to work hard. On the other hand, it is no evidence of an industrious character if a man works hard at the point of a bayonet, or when in danger of losing his job and starving to death. So, with the same more normal inducements of everyday life on a farm, in a factory, or in a family, the persons with an industrious character will accomplish more work than those who are lazy. In a large population there will be found a complete gradation from very high quality to very low quality in each trait of character.

As will be seen, in our present study of personal character I have started with actions which can be observed. This makes a solid tangible foundation. In fact action, as evidence of character, is a good place to start but a poor place to stop. The reason is that when we know only what a man has done, our knowledge omits altogether why he did it—that is, the *motive*. See Lindzey (10). Two men may do exactly the same thing, but from entirely different motives. Knowledge of action only is superficial. So in attempting a judgment of character we should always ask ourselves what motive led to the action taken, and we should whenever possible try to find the answer. If we can add a sound estimate of motives to the knowledge of actions, we greatly increase the value of our knowledge for the purpose of dealing with individuals.

A correct understanding of motives is difficult to come by. Such knowledge must necessarily have an element of uncertainty. It requires more than a knowledge of facts; it requires an understanding of people and situations. Some persons concerned with foreign intelligence or foreign relations do not have this gift. It has been demonstrated that some do have it.

Furthermore, it is well known that a person often acts from mixed motives. Several motives may impel me to quit my job. One of these motives may be very strong—in fact, controlling. Other motives may urge me in the same direction, but have relatively little real importance in my final decision. I may pretend to other people, and perhaps even to myself, that some unimportant motive is the one which is decisive. A good common-sense discussion of motivation is given by Klineberg (18). See also Lindzey, *The Assessment of Human Motives* (10).

Character in Action—An Informal Picture

The following little drama will illustrate informally and more specifically the capabilities and limitations of this concept of character and its utilization when dealing with individuals or nations as we have just presented it. The hero is Mr. H. The neighbors agree that Mr. H is courageous, industrious, generous and trustworthy. The villain is Mr. V, who (we regret to report) is cowardly, lazy, stingy and untrustworthy. What worthwhile meaning can we give to the above statement about the characters of H and V, which sticks the closest to objective facts, and which rests as little as possible on shaky foundations?

I claim that under most of the conditions pertinent to the characteristic in question, the chances are greatly in favor of H being courageous, industrious and generous; and under these same conditions the chances are much against V showing any of these virtues.

Now let us assume that H and V have approximately the same income and the same financial commitments. However, we *know* that H gives large amounts to charity, whereas V gives very little. So far in our discussion we are safe from the criticisms of the psychologist. We have not pretended to know more than we really do.

Now *if* we can go deeper and get at the underlying motives which lead a given person to be generous, we can gain an even greater advantage in our dealings with him. For example, if we know that H gives generously to the Community Chest because he is really sorry for the poor, or on the other hand because he likes to stand well in the sight of the social leaders of the community, then we will know how to make the most effective appeal to him. Also we can learn when to expect a change in his generous actions by watching for changes in the situation through which his motives act.

In the above discussion there is no implication that the commendable or desirable traits of character are usually found together in one individual (or nation). Thus we find individuals who are brave but dishonest; some that are kind but lazy; many that are industrious and stingy.

Operational—Verifiable—Predictable

Modern discussions of the natural or social sciences, or of philosophy, logic or the scientific method emphasize that to be accepted as part of our working knowledge any hypothesis or concept should be, as far as possible, *operational, verifiable,* and a basis for *predictions.* These are high standards. See, for example, *Operational Philosophy* (19).

Returning now to the subject of personal character, a statement appeared some years ago in a book on business administration substantially as follows: "If you are employed for several years in a business office, you will soon know everything that there is to know about the character of your colleagues. Nothing of this sort is hidden from you." [3] When we consider the common traits of character we see that this statement has much truth in it. Consider, for example, such common and vitally important traits as industry, thoroughness, reliability, generosity, loyalty, moral courage, tenacity, will-to-win, initiative, aggressiveness, spirit of fair play, spirit of cooperation, truthfulness, spiritual qualities—and their OPPOSITES.

By working side by side with one's colleagues in periods of stress and in slack times, seeing examples of their work, asking for help and giving help, competing for promotion, dealing with the boss, going out to lunch, and working late in the evenings, perhaps borrowing or lending a little money, collaborating on a project and sharing in the resulting praise or blame—in all of these contacts one learns about personal character. By observing a colleague in many situations and in a whole range of opportunity for loyalty or disloyalty, for fair play or unfair competition, for generosity or selfishness—one gets not only to see the outward behavior resulting in part from the individual's inner character, but also to infer and understand the inner character itself. To go back to our informal definition of personal character, one learns to what extent a colleague will consistently show behavior indicative of industry, generosity, loyalty, moral courage, fair play, and tenacity, beyond what is required to keep him out of serious trouble.

Right away we see that knowledge gained in this way satisfies the exacting criteria for acceptable knowledge given in the title to this subsection. This knowledge of character is *operational:* you can do something about it, and others do something to you as a direct result of their character as herein understood. It is *verifiable:* to verify generosity you can ask for help. It is *predictable:* from some colleagues you expect (predict) careful work, tenacity in sticking to a difficult problem, straightforward treatment of competitors for promotion. You can check to see if your predictions come true. I repeat that all of these observations are carried out under a wide range of conditions. I make no claim that from a given colleague a certain type of behavior *always* occurs.

We see from such observations that most of our knowledge of personal character seems to be reliable. This knowledge is open to any intelligent man who has opportunities for frequent contacts with others. It requires no occult ability in mind reading. Furthermore it requires no technical knowledge of psychology or anthropology. The usableness of this knowledge of personal character does not depend upon any particular assumptions, definitions or theories derived from psychology, anthropology, or the other social or non-social sciences.

This common-sense understanding of personal character can be gained to a greater or less degree by anyone who does not have the particularly favorable opportunities just described, provided he is really interested in people other than himself. This proviso is important also for those who are supposed to gain a knowledge of national character, e.g., U.S. Foreign Service representatives on a foreign assignment. Some can live in a foreign country for years without learning anything about the people. Certainly a thirst for knowledge is the beginning of wisdom. Such nonscientific understanding of personal character described in this section is, of course, put to practical use by nearly everyone every day in his personal relations.

From this consideration of personal character we can proceed by logical steps to a consideration of national character, as we shall now see. Personal character forms part of the foundation of national character, but it is only a part of the picture. To understand national character and especially the *applications* of our knowledge of national character to international relations and foreign intelligence, we have a more difficult problem. We seek now all the help that we can get from social psychology, cultural anthropology and from the many excellent workers in these and related fields.

SCIENTIFIC ASPECTS OF PERSONAL AND GROUP CHARACTER

Personal character is a fact of life with which everyone is more or less familiar from his own day-to-day experience. It is so close to us that anyone can learn something at least about this subject merely by considering his own character, with its strengths, weaknesses, its unity, conflicts and inconsistencies.

To extend our definite and helpful ideas of *individual character* so as to form a concept of *group character* is in some ways a natural, logical, and useful extension. Yet it also involves many difficulties. There may be proper doubts as to the soundness of our assumptions. There are certainly questions as to the new meanings of terms which were originally intended to apply only to individual character. There are practical difficulties as to means for gaining a knowledge of the character of a group and the best way to express what we have learned.

In the face of these difficulties we look for help wherever help may be found. Our first source of help is naturally the common-sense point of view, namely, the practical observations of practical men who have been dealing with various groups, peoples and nations for many years and have described some of the differences in character in simple, nonscientific operational terms of varying reliability and involving conclusions of varying degrees of soundness. See, for example, the publications described in Section 9 and listed in the Supplement to the Bibliography of this book. Many of these are of great value. A second source of help is that of the scientist. Group or national character was originally the field of the psychologist and the cultural anthropologist. Contributions to our understanding of the character of groups of human beings are now also being made by political scientists, sociologists and even by some historians. All who have to do with international relations, including those in the foreign service and in foreign intelligence, now have to take some position regarding the meaning and importance of group and national character.

Scientific Explanations of Character

For the purposes of the present book, what have the various scientists to offer toward an understanding of character which will be sound and practically helpful in the production of foreign intelligence and in all dealings with foreign peoples?

For some three thousand years historians have reported facts which can be considered to throw light on the differing character of peoples. In the past century or so systematic studies have been made of primitive civilizations, mostly by anthropologists. At the same time studies of individual character—intended to be scientific—were made by psychologists. Much of this was pioneering research, and like all pioneering research it involved much trial and error, with emphasis on the latter word. All of this is clearly described by Potter (20, pp. 10-66).

As a result of excellent work by many, a reasonably sound and well-supported picture of the bases of personal, group and national character has now appeared. A simplified [1] version of the scientific side of this picture follows, much of this being taken from Potter (20). In later sections of this book I discuss the human aspects of the picture and the applications to foreign affairs.

An excellent start is presented by Kluckhohn and Murray (21) who say: "Every man is in certain respects:

a) like all other men [his basic human inheritance]
b) like some other men [resulting from their common inborn and environmental influences]
c) like no other men [his individuality]." [2]

We logically begin our study with an individual's inherited, inborn qualities. These inborn qualities set the limits to which any individual can rise in certain activities provided all the surrounding circumstances are most favorable.

Recent critical studies by Kluckhohn and others have shown that the *distribution* of inborn mental qualities is remarkably uniform, as between races, ethnic groups or other large human aggregations. We have to abandon (perhaps reluctantly) a large part of our former ideas of inborn superiorities in groups or races. The undoubted superiority of some peoples in some activities is now attributed to the ever present, ever active, and almost insidious effect of the culture of the group into which a person is born, acting on an individual directly or indirectly during all the waking moments of his life. As someone said, if we were deep-sea denizens, probably the last important factor in our environment which we should fully appreciate as such would be water. For a human being, culture is as omnipresent and inescapable as water to a deep-sea fish.

All of the elements of a human being's cultural environment influence his development, or may influence it, directly or indirectly from birth.

Physical environment includes food, weather and type of terrain in which he lives. Here again the influence of physical environment is now down-graded in favor of personal environment, including culture. It has been well said that modern culture builds a shield between an individual and his physical environment; e.g., he may live in a cold climate but in a warm house. The shield is far from perfect, of course.

Personality

The central theme of the modern scientific point of view is that culture acting on inborn qualities develops each individual's personality. *Personality* and *culture* continually acting and interacting upon each other are among the basic factors in the development of human individuals and human institutions.

Personality has now acquired in the behavioral sciences a very broad and rather definite meaning. For an individual it includes all of man's mental, moral and spiritual qualities. Kluckhohn and Murray (21A) sum this up when they say (p. 6): "The superordinate governing institution of the human organism is the *personality*, or mind. Its main physiological and neurological basis lies in the head. . . . Thus the psychologist is directly concerned only with the manifestations of the personality, *the facts*. . . . Hence the personality is an abstract formulation composed by the psychologist." These authors discuss in detail the modern concept of personality as used in the present study. Such details are interesting but are not considered necessary for our purposes.

As one other fruitful contribution toward our understanding of personality, we should mention Adorno's *The Authoritarian Personality* (22), which points out the value of viewing a personality as a whole.

Culture

Culture has an equally broad meaning.[3] I shall follow the excellent example of Potter in that I will not here make the mistake of attempting any one definition. Potter (20) says: "Ralph Linton [23] spoke of culture simply as 'the way of life in any society.' . . . 'Societies are organized groups of individuals, and cultures are, in the last analysis, nothing more than the organized repetitive responses of a society's members.'" According to Potter, Linton also defined culture as "social heredity" and he says: "a consensus of behavior and opinion constitutes a cultural pattern."

The same general ideas from a different point of view are presented by Kluckhohn and Murray (21, p. 54): "Human beings, however, learn not only from experience but also from each other. All human societies rely greatly for their survival upon accumulated learning (culture). Culture is a great storehouse of ready-made solutions to problems which human animals are wont to encounter. This storehouse is man's substitute for instinct. It is filled not merely with pooled learning of the living members of the society, but also with the learning of men long dead and of men belonging to other societies."

No one can "react to [all of] the countless number of stimuli which the environment projects upon him." So again, "the concept of culture . . ." presents the culture as a screen or filter which bars some of the conditions in the environment and prevents them from having any impact upon the personality or even upon the consciousness, while it admits the stimuli of certain other conditions and even amplifies their strength as stimuli."

Potter sums up: "Culture, the medium, and personality, the receptor, were indispensable, each to the other." See also Malinowski (23A).

The same element of cultural pressure, acting on two different individuals under the same outward conditions, may have markedly different effects in their behaviors. This is said to be due to the differences in their personalities at the time of the pressure. The differences in personalities at that time involve two factors, namely the differences in their inborn traits, and the different cultural influences to which each has been subjected since birth. To these two may be added what Kluckhohn and Murray call "situational determinants," meaning special situations not of direct cultural origin, such as a serious illness, involvement in a railroad wreck.

So if two individuals are suddenly confronted with exactly the same danger, say a sudden storm in a small sailboat, to one it may be a stimulating and thrilling experience, to the other an unnerving and depressing occasion.

Determinants

An individual's personality is viewed as being based upon his inborn qualities, but it is not a fixed quantity. His personality is constantly receiving pressures from his physical environment and from other human beings (each one with his own culture), and from other aspects of the culture into which the individual is born. Thus an individual's personality is subject to change, depending upon the personality-forming influences which impinge upon it, and it does so change from the cradle to the grave. Personality is influenced also by the normal biological processes associated with growth and aging.

The influences of all kinds which react upon an individual from birth to death and which so modify his personality (and his character) are technically called *determinants*. In their discussion I have called them personality-forming or character-forming influences. Kluckhohn and Murray have divided these determinants into four categories, with elaborate explanations which I present in simplified form:

1. "Constitutional Determinants"

   This category comprises the inherited qualities as modified by environment, such as food, climate, etc. It includes sex, age, health, appearance, potentialities for learning, for energy level, frustration tolerance.

2. "Group Membership Determinants"

   Those influences derived from membership in certain groups which may or may not be overlapping. The influences which are distinctive for each group arise from the distinctive elements of that group's culture. This category includes actions, values, motives. Consistency in the culture of a group adds an element of predictability to the actions of its members.

3. "Role Determinants"

   Roles here mean how the functions necessary to group life are performed. How other members of the group expect a role to be performed is also important. Each man has his role in his group, large or small, as leader, priest, school teacher, father of a family, etc.

4. "Situational Determinants"

These are special "accidental" occurrences which happen to an individual from time to time and are not part of any regular cultural or other pattern. Some such special situations may be sickness, auto accidents, unusual contacts with people who influence the individual, etc.

It is evident that these four types of determinants are interdependent, and influence one another.

Gorer (24) makes the particularly illuminating point that: "National character also refers to the *ideal image of themselves* in the light of which individuals assess and pass judgment upon themselves and their neighbors, and on the basis of which they reward and punish their children, for the manifestation or nonmanifestation of given traits and attitudes." (Emphasis added.)

In continental Europe in the time of Louis XIV the ideal was the courtier; in England of the nineteenth century the ideal was the country squire; in America of the early 1800's the ideal was the pioneer. Each set a goal which influenced the character of many, even though few could themselves actually attain to the position of a courtier, or a country squire, or a pioneer.

Character as One Aspect of Personality

Personality is, as I have said, a very broad concept consisting of many traits. Some of these traits are rather superficial and temporary. Some of the others, which are usually more permanent and deep-seated, are the traits which we associate with the word "character" as already described. They are associated with such well-known and well-understood traits of individual character as honesty, industry, generosity, tenacity, aggressiveness, courage, etc. The science of psychology has not advanced to the point where it can provide us with any definition of character which would make us any wiser than we now are for the purposes of this study. Nothing would be gained by attempting to frame or find a definition which would have the superficial appearance of being "scientific."

As we all know, there are many character-forming influences, and character, like personality, changes as a result of the impact of culture, environment, and special personal experiences. We have all seen people increase or decrease in their degree of honesty, industry, generosity.

I have defined an honest, industrious or generous man, or man of any other character, as one who voluntarily shows more of the qualities of the character in question than he has to in order to keep himself out of serious trouble.

GROUP CHARACTER—
PRACTICAL WORKINGS

Where do these common sense observations and these latest scientific developments leave the concept of group or national character? Have the observations described in Section 3 and the scientific developments which I have just outlined tended to discredit or to strengthen this concept? It seems appropriate to consider the question here, even though it anticipates a part of what appears later in this book.

Riesman, as already quoted in Section 2, states the situation and the point of view which seems to me most useful for the present study.

Potter (20, pp. 41 and 57) with whom I concur puts the case:

After all its vicissitudes, national character is still with us. The fact is inescapable. . . . I believe it is entirely just to say that these new investigations have reaffirmed the concept of national character and have successfully met most of the difficulties which I discussed previously. First of all, they have been at great pains to demonstrate, at the purely expository level, that uniformities of attitude and behavior actually exist and thus that *national character is verifiable as a factual reality.* Second, by their attention to the culture they have explored the medium within which national character develops and have provided a basis for regarding it, as it should be regarded, as a relative rather than as an absolute quality, altering gradually in response to changing conditions and manifesting itself as a *tendency in the majority of members of the national group* rather than as a universal attribute present in all of them. . . . (Emphasis added).

See also Sir Harold Nicolson (24A), the distinguished British diplomat, Member of Parliament and author, who states his firm belief in the importance of national character. He says, "There does remain a sufficiently recognizable, a sufficiently permanent element in the national character to render it something stable and something that affects policy, that almost governs policy." [1]

The foregoing discussions of the scientific background of the concepts of group and national character will provide a rational foundation for the practical discussions which are to follow. The scientific status of this subject and especially the still-existing shortcomings of the social sciences involved are summed up in Appendix D.

Groups Described

The groups of which we shall now speak are usually much smaller than a nation. A nation may still be considered as a group, but of a special type. There are many kinds of groups and they may be either organized or unorganized. Examples are: political parties, trade unions, farmers' groups, churches, a university, a scientific or professional society such as the American Medical Association or the American Bar Association, trade associations, a town or even a geographical area the inhabitants of which have important interests in common. Many groups are of the type commonly known as pressure groups. In each group the members have some one or more interests in common. This is the unifying feature of a group.

In developing our basis for discussing the very large general subject of national character, these groups represent, as we shall see, rather satisfying units on which to tie our concepts of character and the mechanisms of political action. They are an important part of the mechanism of national action.

A fuller discussion of the kinds of nations and groups and the significance of definitions in this field is given in Appendix A, "Some Characteristics of Nations and Smaller Groups."

In view of the importance of groups in national behavior and in so much of the political, social, and economic life of a nation, it is worthwhile to go a little more deeply into their life and procedures, and the factors which usually make for growth and vigor, or the reverse. In the active pursuit of foreign intelligence production, or in our effort to understand a specific international situation, we may often identify some groups which are the keys to the outcome of the situation before us. These may be groups friendly to our interests, or they may be groups opposed to what we consider the best interests of the United States. Any of these groups may exist in our own country, or in a friendly, neutral or hostile nation.

Much has been written about groups because they are such an important influence on individual character. Sorokin's book of *Society, Culture and Personality, Their Structure and Dynamics* (25) contains over 300,000 words entirely devoted to the subject of groups. For an excellent readable discussion see Snyder and Wilson (26). A briefer and more straightforward statement of what has been called "group dynamics" is given in Chapter 17 on "The Individual in the Group" in Klineberg's *Social Psychology* (18) already mentioned.

What are some of the factors which generally make for group progress, and what are some of the symptoms of group weakness?

A group may exist in hostile surroundings where it must fight against attempts to suppress it (like the Mafia in the United States); or it may have more or less friendly rivals (like a business, professional or religious rival) which may crowd it out of existence; or it may have a monopoly of its field and no opposition. Even in this last case the group must compete for the time and dues of its members, otherwise it may dry up and die of inactivity. So *all* groups—like other living organisms—must constantly *compete* in some way for their existence and for the active support of their members.

Groups, being relatively small and intimate as compared with a nation, are more quickly responsive to the influence of a single leader, or of a small controlling faction. Upon a change in the leadership, a group may rapidly increase or decrease in size and power, and even in the direction of its efforts. Groups that survive for many years often show several recurring periods of expansion and decline.

All groups have certain general principles for which they are supposed to exist (called by Lasswell and Kaplan the "principled interests"). They have also their "expediency interests."

For example, the American Chemical Society may have as its "principled interest" to advance the science of chemistry; but it also has an "expediency interest" to advance (perhaps indirectly) the well-being of its members in prestige and salary.

As might be expected, groups having interests which

are sharply focused usually have more solidarity and vigor than those whose interests are diffuse. Opposition is often helpful to a group by increasing the loyalty and solidarity of its members.

Lasswell and Kaplan (27) have an excellent chapter on groups as part of their rather complete system of political theory. Their definitions and propositions are rigorous and abstract. Their chapter on groups, and their whole book devoted to political theory, will add greatly to the knowledge and understanding of those concerned with the inner mechanisms and external actions of nations. Such understanding is evidently a prerequisite for estimates of any future developments in which groups would play a significant part. As one definition and brief discussion out of many which in a few words throws much light on the inner working of groups I select the following:

> Co-operation is the integration of diversified operations; solidarity, of diversified thinking.
> . . . Co-operation then is "doing" together; solidarity is "thinking" and "feeling" together.

From Individual Character to Group Character

When we extend our consideration of the character of an individual to the character of a group, we are evidently stretching some concepts, as we have already pointed out, beyond their original meaning. Strictly speaking, only an individual has a mind, feels a sense of pride or shame. But when speaking conveniently, meaningfully and usefully rather than strictly, we find it very common to speak of the American Mind (28), the Academic Mind (29), the Mind of Germany (29A). Ginsberg (16) states that "*the group or national mind is* not a mind in the sense in which this term is used when applied to an organism possessed of a unitary center of consciousness, but rather *a mental condition widely dominating thought and action.*" The latter phrase makes a good working definition. He speaks also of "the collective life of a nation." His whole book has unusual value for this study, partly because of his emphasis on the collective aspects of national character.

We have all been members of some group which has just achieved some special triumph. The sense of pride of each member present was greater and different than it would have been had he been alone. The pride of each member interacted with and reinforced the pride of the other members, so that the group as a whole could properly be said to have a sense of pride of its own, different in kind from the sum total of the separate feelings of each individual when alone. Similarly in discouragement or even more in panic, the total feeling in the group is much greater than, and different from, the sum of what the individual feelings would be if each individual were alone. This is well brought out by Snow (30).

The effects of mob psychology can be witnessed to some degree in the rapid spread of some mental epidemic which seems to sweep through an otherwise sane people like a disease, even when they are not all in one place. Examples are the outburst of witch-hunting in New England in colonial times and the mildly similar search for disloyal persons and the burning of (allegedly subversive) books during the spread of "McCarthyism." Viewed in the seclusion of retrospect the extreme absurdities of such group hysteria are humiliating and seem almost unbelievable. Such episodes do throw light on group action. It *can* happen here.

Examples of irrational optimism are the South Sea Bubble and most of the prolonged bull markets. An example of irrational panic was the celebrated *Grande*

Peur which swept rural France in the summer of 1789. Rumors about troop movements, exaggerated fears that the Crown and the aristocracy plotted a massacre of the peasantry, when added to the hardships of famine, all led to an orgy of violence on the French countryside—with the sacking of chateaux, violence to officials and estate officers.

Of course individuals differ in the degree to which they lose their personalities in a crowd. Some have more critical ability than others. This trait is related to inner-directed, other-directed, and tradition-directed as proposed by Riesman (12) as the useful categories of human beings. All of this is a commonplace of social psychology. In general, a crowd is more primitive in its group character than the members who compose it. We are not here principally concerned with the extreme manifestations of panic or cruelty.

Certainly a group acting as a whole can exhibit types of behavior similar to those associated with traits of individual character. For example: generosity, in voting a contribution to charity; courage, in opposing as a group some persons in authority; conservatism, in voting against change.

Fouillée (31) points out that the good qualities of a people are as a rule more deeply hidden than the vices and absurdities, which latter catch public attention.

As a matter of fact, we find that *many groups*—small as compared with a nation—*develop a well-recognized character and maintain it consistently through many generations.* As six examples among very many which could be mentioned: (a) The Massachusetts Institute of Technology has long maintained its high character as a leader in giving the best type of engineering education. (b) In the Roman Catholic Church the Society of Jesus has maintained its typical character of aggressive Christianity.

(c) The First Division of the United States Army in World Wars I and II maintained its character for "a special pride of service and a high state of morale never broken by hardship nor battle" (32)—this in spite of frequent changes of commanders and many changes in other personnel due to enormous casualties. (d) In Tammany Hall much of the original group character remains. Turning now to groups other than institutions or similar closely knit organizations we may note as further examples of the persistence of certain traits of character for a considerable period of time in a group. (e) The German Officer Corps. It is remarkable that this group originally based on the Prussian Army was able until 1945 to maintain its character and to maintain its standards, traditions and aristocratic characteristics of thought and behavior, while drawing its recruits for some seventy-five years mainly from non-Prussian and non-aristocratic sources. (f) Finally we may consider that entity which seems vague at a cursory glance, namely, the completely informal, loosely knit and widespread British Establishment [2] (33). The Establishment, until recently drawn almost exclusively from the Upper Classes (the capitals are meaningful), has now been able to recruit a large proportion of its membership from the middle classes and still to maintain its essential characteristics in large measure.

Groups and the foregoing aspects of group character are justified for detailed consideration here, first to show that the leap from individual character to group character is not as unwarranted as it might seem at first glance; second, because in many respects the character and resultant behavior of a nation when acting as a whole—that is, as a nation—may often conveniently be considered as the result of the interaction of groups within the nation (such groups as farmers, trade unions, the

Irish); third, because everyone is familiar, from his own personal experience, with the character and behavior of the small groups to which he belongs and so can visualize the reactions described here. Riesman (34) sums this up when he says, "Institutions [which are a form of group] mediate between the family and society."

The Interactions of Individual and Group Character

The influence of groups is of two quite different kinds. First, when the influence extends *inward*, the group is one of the most important influences in the formation of the character of the individuals within the group. Second, when the influence extends *outward* from the group, groups are one of the most important influences in the formation of the character of the nation when acting as a nation.

In most of the groups considered here, there are many opportunities for a member to influence the group, and vice versa. Many of the groups are small enough so that members come into frequent personal contact with one another. Klineberg (18, p. 438) uses for such the illuminating term, "the face-to-face group." Most national organizations (trade unions, professional societies, religious and cultural organizations, for example) have local chapters where even humble members may be seen and heard. The action of a local chapter naturally influences the action of the national group organization. Many organizations have a publication to which a member may contribute articles. Through all these means an active individual can easily make his influence felt.

On the other hand there are many opportunities for the group to influence the members. A member of a group may receive character-forming influences from the group, either from other members in personal discussions, or from the group as such in the form of official communications, including the group publications. In many cases the indirect influence of the group on its members may be exerted through the dissemination of ideas within the group by many different channels. There is in fact no stronger influence acting upon most individuals than the social pressure exerted by a group like a small closely knit community, in which members live and make personal contacts every day.

Secondary schools, especially the schools called "private" in the United States and "public" in England, are ideally situated for influencing the character of the pupils. Such schools make specific and repeated claims as character-forming institutions in their literature.

In regard to dissident minorities within a group Ginsberg says: "Institutions may not reflect the character of all the members, but perhaps only of powerful sections, and once formed they [the groups] tend to select the type that suits them. In this way many qualities in a population may remain dormant or repressed until a change of circumstances brings them into play or revolutions may be reactions against a group unduly dominant. Thus it is possible for revolutionary changes to take place in institutions without a parallel change in the underlying quality of the mass of the nation" (16). In other words many revolutions do not indicate a change in the character of the people involved. They indicate only that traits of character long suppressed have at last found means of expression. The practical importance of this well-known fact is that United States representatives in a foreign country must get below the surface in order to understand the potential forces which may gain expression. Current examples are Cuba and the large number of former colonies which have recently sought and gained independence.

The *mutual* influence of members of a group upon one another and upon the group as a whole, and in turn the influence of the group as a whole upon the members, have been the happy hunting grounds of the social psychologists. As one example, Klineberg (18, Chapter on "The Individual and the Group") indicates some of the principal topics to be considered by his use of the following headings: group communications, imitation, suggestion, mob reaction, social facilitation, conformity, group dynamics, leadership. Much very reliable work, practically useful to the intelligence officer, has been done in this field. Lasswell and Kaplan (27, p. 44) describe the stages through which a group typically passes in the course of its growth and development.

Leadership and The Elites

Leadership in a group constitutes one of the significant opportunities for a member to influence the group. What is said of group leadership applies also to the very large associations of human beings, such as peoples and nations.

Closely related to leadership is the concept of the elite. Much has been written recently about the elite.[3] A definition and explanation which differentiates "elite" from "leader" is given in *The Comparative Study of Elites* (36) as follows:

> A leader is ordinarily supposed to be a prominent and active person. All leaders collectively are the "leadership." What is lacking is a term to cover both leadership and the strata of society from which leaders usually come. Consider Winston Churchill. No one hesitates to call him a leader and to recognize that he has been part of the leadership of England for a long time, even though he was not always a leader. Nevertheless, even when too young to take part in

public affairs, Churchill belonged to the political elite of his country, since he was born into one of the ruling families.

The concept of the elite . . . [designates] the holders of high positions in a given society. There are as many elites as there are values. Besides an elite of power (the political elite) there are elites of wealth, respect, and knowledge (to name but a few). Since we need a term for persons who are elite in relation to several values we speak of "the elite" (the elite society). In democratic countries the political elite is recruited from a broad base. Elites in non-democratic societies, on the contrary, spring from a narrow base, often from a few families.

The elite in a group are apt to be those with the most power, the mass those with the least power. Likewise the elite have the most privileges, whether salary, deference or otherwise. The elite are "the privileged few" [4] as contrasted with the (not necessarily underprivileged) "many."

The division between the elite and the mass can be made wherever there are any differences . . . in the amount of priority enjoyed by various persons in the group. . . . No more than this is contained in such assertions as Pareto's that "every people is governed by an elite, by a chosen element in the population"; what is said, in effect, is that every people is ruled by—rulers.

It is not the existence of the limited group, but the method of its establishment which serves as the essential criterion of the several forms of government.

Upper elites tend to be skilled in the practices of interpersonal relations rather than of the area in which decisions are being made.[5]

The elite have the power of decision and the power to implement their decisions. This latter helps to determine whether or not a specific policy is in fact a decision. They should have the skills necessary for their jobs, should be fairly representative, and should be accountable to the citizens, stockholders, or members whom they are supposed to serve.

Ginsburg (16) quotes an interesting statement by Fouillée, "If you leave out of consideration the elite of France, there is no more France; France is reduced to the level of those people who have no history." See also *The Comparative Study of Elites* (36).

Elites are important in any consideration of national character for the reasons already given under leadership. Elites are also important because (as explained in Section 4) many men use the elite of their own group as the model upon which they try to shape the characters of themselves and their children. Finally, data on the elite of a foreign country is largely knowable and can usually be obtained by diplomatic and intelligence services. Changes in the elite are often excellent indications of the approach of other changes which might not otherwise be noticed. These changes may include changes, perhaps incipient changes, in national character. (See Section 12.)

In estimating the action which will be taken by a group in the near future it is often necessary to know two factors: What the leaders want; and to what extent the members will co-operate.[6]

One of the most important aspects of the mode of operation of a group, political or other, is the means by which the leaders transmit their own reactions convincingly and effectively to the rank and file within the group. These means may range all the way from pure compulsion to the "purest" form of democracy, with free discussion, a secret ballot and majority rule. Here, as is so often the case in human relations, the real operations—including the underlying pressures and the off-the-record deals—are more important than the public record and the printed regulations or constitution.

In some cases well-known in history, the operations described above are reversed, so that the masses impose their ideas—almost their demands—upon the leaders.

In a given group the opportunities for attaining leadership and the classes from which leaders are selected are important elements in estimating the present and future character of a group in a foreign country and the probable character of its members. If, for example, selection of leaders is limited by heredity, or wealth, or to a certain college or religion or clique, such limitation would be significant in estimating group character. For similar reasons information about the stability of the present administration of the group is significant. If the leadership is due for a change, who are the likely successors? Is there a dissatisfied minority which is seeking power?

The Influence of Leadership on the Range of Character

As leadership has many impacts on the respective characters of individuals, small groups and nations, it will now be appropriate to consider the constant interaction between leadership and character.[7] In this case both individual and group character are affected.

Examples of the striking results of leadership in history are well known. Peter the Great, Napoleon, Hitler, Washington, Lincoln and many others each imposed elements of his own personal character on the history of his times. The reader can supply an equally imposing array of leaders who have left their marks on religion, education, science, literature, philosophy, or other fields.

A study of the leaders of groups of all sizes and in all

ages demonstrates that leaders certainly exert a tremendous influence on the actions of their followers and seem-
ingly also eventually on their character.[8] It is pertinent
to examine now in detail the mechanism of such influence.

In any large group, the membership of which has not
already been specially selected, the range of intensity
of any trait of individual character will probably extend
from very high to very low. The degree to which an individual possesses any given trait of character may be
estimated by the amount of pressure required to cause
the individual to manifest that trait, or sometimes the
amount of pressure required to induce him to manifest
the opposite character. Thus for most of us, some little
urging is necessary to cause us to give money to a charity,
so we could estimate the degree of generosity by the
amount of pressure required (other things being equal).[9]
However, in considering such a type of character as
honesty, it does not require any appreciable inducement
to cause most of us to be honest. The measurement here
would be rated in the reverse direction. How much of an
inducement is required to make us act dishonestly? For
example, most of us would steal to prevent our children
from starving to death if there was no other alternative.

This concept of *a whole spectrum* of degrees of each
trait of individual character is true to life, and is very
helpful in getting a usable picture of the characters of
any group of individuals in regard to any trait of character.[10] As an example of the varying degrees of any trait
of character in any group, and as a demonstration of the
varying amounts of pressure required by different people
to induce them to manifest a certain trait of character,
consider a group of people, all of whom have agreed to
attend a meeting on a certain night to assist in a certain
project, let us say to go out to solicit funds or votes. We
know that the least threat of rain will keep some away

from the meeting and so from carrying out their promise. Others would be kept away by a bad storm; and there are some who are such fanatics that nothing less than an earthquake or a blizzard will keep them away from an activity in which they have promised to participate.

So with every other trait of character. Each man, according to his character, may have a high, low or medium *degree* of honesty, industry, generosity, etc., as is evidenced by the amount of pressure required to make him act honestly, industriously, generously—or if more convenient, in any special case the inverse of the amount of pressure which will *prevent* him from acting in a given way.

This is a matter of everyday experience. It is a point of view essential to understanding group character. When the going gets a little tough a certain percentage of the weak sisters falls away. When it gets tougher another percentage falls away. There are usually a small number who are surprisingly weak and another small number who are surprisingly dedicated at each end of the range for any character in any group.

At the upper extreme of dedication to the cause in any large group we may find 1 per cent or less who have sufficient character to go the whole way. In religious conviction such a person will be burned at the stake rather than recant; in courage he will remain and fight to certain death, even when he could honorably retreat. There is another small percentage, say 9 per cent,[11] who will go to great lengths in support of their religion or in combat, though not to certain death "beyond the call of duty." Finally let us say that at the bottom of the scale there are 10 per cent who have no loyalty to any religion, are hopeless cowards, or are shamelessly lazy. This leaves about 80 per cent $\pm$ 30 per cent in the middle who will generally bow to whatever authority may be in power, will float with the prevailing current, and can be counted upon eventually to follow the line of least resistance regardless of their personal convictions. Thus in Tudor England when the official religion changed from Protestantism under Edward VI to Catholicism under Mary, and back to Protestantism under Elizabeth I, all within little more than five years, some few were martyrs to the cause of their religion. A large number nominally changed religion twice in five years according to the reigning sovereign. Again in France and many other European countries during their occupation by Germany in World War II, some few nationals bravely joined the resistance movements, but the great majority continued in "business as usual." If they were shopkeepers, or what you will, they served the Germans in occupation almost as readily as they served their own fellow countrymen.

This middle 80 per cent varied greatly within itself. Those near the bottom complied willingly and without trouble. Others resisted their unwelcome rulers and the laws with which they did not agree for a time with passive disobedience or otherwise. But the point is that the enormous majority succumbed to the pressure in time without the necessity of criminal prosecutions or executions.

So most people will go along with the prevailing opinion without thinking much for themselves or without displaying much of either courage or energy in going against the crowd. By cajolery and by using many kinds of mild economic or social pressure or perhaps by the inspiration of his leadership, a good leader can induce the great majority of his flock to follow him. Thus a skilful leader in a position of leadership over a group of average men can cause them to exhibit achievement far above the average in giving (generosity); in work accomplished (industry); in fighting qualities (courage); in refusal to quit (tenacity). This type of leadership if continued consistently over many years, especially over a generation (twenty-five years) or more, may result in a habit and a tradition of courage (as in Sparta) or tenacity (as the British). It is highly probable that habit, accompanied by the appropriate political atmosphere and propaganda, can be a character-forming influence. We tend to accept without conscious decision or thought what we see everybody doing.

Thus it is *certain* from everyday experience that a good leader can multiply many times the overt actions, such as giving, fighting, physical work, usually considered as the results of character. It is *probable* that such influences when long continued will result in habits and traditions, and that these will eventually have a significant effect on the real character of persons, groups and nations. Leadership may verge into compulsion. It is probable that such influences on character are presently being exerted to an unprecedented extent in the U.S.S.R., and in the Soviet satellites, and in Communist China, as described later.

The Force of Compulsion

Social, political and economic pressure to induce a man to perform more or less of some activity than he would otherwise do are common in all nations and in all social units from the family up. When such pressures are carried to the extreme the pressure is known as compulsion. The compulsion that we are now talking about is the kind that has become common in the Communist countries. It is the kind exerted by the secret police by which a man who honestly opposes some government policy may be removed from his home without trial and may disappear into a prison camp in Siberia. It is the kind of compulsion which may lead to a man's being dispossessed of his farm, or expelled from his job and excluded from finding any other means of earning a living, so that he and his family starve. It is the sort of compulsion which may end in purges and executions.

Such methods seldom exist today in the nations of the free world. They are almost foreign to the experience and the thoughts of Americans. It is, therefore, difficult for us to realize the long-continued effect of this kind of compulsion from all sides—and where there is no escape —upon the actions of a whole people, and eventually upon their character. There is no doubt that this sort of compulsion, when ruthlessly applied, can accomplish impressive results if not miracles *over a period of years*. It has certainly caused some changes in the activities of the Communist Chinese which are at variance with the character of the Chinese as heretofore known. It is the only explanation for some developments which have taken place in the U.S.S.R. and for many activities now carried out by the puppet governments of the Soviet satellites.

The effect of compulsion and the constant threat thereof behind the Iron Curtain is a force which we should never overlook. Few persons have the character to stand against it year after year.

The Soviet atmosphere of constant and all-pervading pressure to adhere to the party line is vividly brought out by Cantril (38A), who quotes liberally from the speeches and writings of the Soviet party leaders. In the last few years the threat of imprisonment or execution for Soviet nationals has greatly diminished. Under present conditions the pressure, as shown by Cantril's examples, is the equally powerful threat of social, political and economic ostracism. One who openly opposes the party doctrine has literally no place to go, for himself or his family. He suffers from a sense of great loneliness. There is in the U.S.S.R. no "loyal opposition." Few can withstand this form of pressure, when exerted on all sides for several generations.

Cantril raises an interesting question as to whether pressure of this type can affect inner conviction and character. I am of the opinion that for most people it does do so within the meanings given in the present book. A clear-cut decision hinges largely on agreed definitions of what is meant by conviction and character. Such definitions would be profitable subjects for discussion elsewhere.

Machiavelli describes the use of compulsion as follows (*The Prince*, VI, 5):

> The nature of the people is mutable; it is easy to persuade them of anything, but difficult to keep them in that persuasion. Hence the prophet should be so well prepared that when they no longer believe he can make them believe by force. (Cited by Lasswell and Kaplan, p. 276.)

BASIC BELIEFS
OR FUNDAMENTAL
PHILOSOPHY[1]

Many of the traits of character which we have been discussing so far are closely related to some behavior which everyone can see and understand. Thus, generosity manifests itself in giving, and courage may be demonstrated by putting up a good fight. But in each nation (or people) there are some traits of character which are more deeply rooted and are related to that people's fundamental concepts about themselves and about nature.

Thus each nation or people has a set of basic beliefs or elements of its fundamental philosophy which can be regarded as traits of character of a special kind. These can helpfully be used as a part of the general concept of national character. When properly understood they offer one of the best means for comprehending the character of a given nation. When overlooked, they present one of the most dangerous sources for misunderstanding in international relations.

The examples of basic beliefs given below all refer to the present time unless otherwise stated.

57

In the United States:

    All men are created free and equal.

    Each side has a right to a fair hearing.

    A man is presumed to be innocent until proven guilty.

For a European gentlemen of the eighteenth century:

    Belief in a technical code of honor (including the obligation to fight duels to defend one's honor).

For the ancient Greeks:

    The wisdom of consulting the omens before making an important decision.

For many barbaric tribes of a few centuries ago:

    The value of human sacrifices.

For most educated men in Western Europe during the Middle Ages:

    The necessity to have only one Christian church.

For additional examples from many countries, including those in Asia and Latin America, see Northrup (42), whose work is discussed later in this section.

From these examples it will be seen that some basic beliefs stem directly from religion. Many do not. A vigorous and appealing slogan, like those just quoted for the United States, often helps to fix and to disseminate a basic belief.

Ortega (39) explains the essence of such beliefs with much insight when he says:

> A belief must be distinguished from an accepted idea, a scientific truth, for instance. Ideas are open to discussion; they convince by virtue of reason; whereas a belief can neither be challenged nor, strictly speaking, defended. While we hold a belief, *it constitutes the very reality in which we live and move and have our being.*

A belief in the strict sense of my terminology is unlikely

to occur as belief of individuals or particular groups. Since it is not a mere opinion, an idea, or a theory, it will normally be of a collective nature. *People are inclined to believe in company* and not of their own accord. A belief functions when established in a social environment by virtue of its "collective validity"—that is, regardless of the adherence of individuals, persons or groups. (Emphasis is mine.)

In other words, for most persons who hold one of these basic beliefs, the belief is so basic that the believer has always assumed its fundamental truth. He has never heard it fundamentally defended or attacked. Most people, not being of an analytical turn of mind, have never heard or formulated for themselves a justification of one of their own basic beliefs. If some one challenges it, the believer finds considerable difficulty in putting his ideas together to defend it. Although such a belief is not necessarily religious, its practice is certainly largely an act of faith.

When we are negotiating with a group or nation, a proposal that fits in with existing beliefs starts with a great advantage. On the other hand, a reasonable proposal which, unknown to the proposer, runs counter to the basic beliefs of the group, experiences difficulties which may seem quite unreasonable to the proposer. In some cases the believer may not even be conscious of the fact that his opposition arises from some basic belief; the connection may not be evident to him.

The deep layer of the character of a people which is represented by its basic beliefs or fundamental philosophy has both reality and unity in its meaning and in its effects. However, there is no English word or simple phrase which expresses this concept fully and satisfactorily. It will facilitate our understanding to consider the following terms, phrases or statements. Each of these presents some aspect of this concept with more or less exactness. The points of view are helpfully different. By taking a look at all of them we arrive at an understanding of this concept. (The emphasis is mine in each case.)

Deeply *entrenched attitudes of thought* and behavior.[2]

The premises on which civilized cultures are built.[3]

Every people has its characteristic set of *primitive postulates.*[4]

The *social psychology* of a people.[5]

Characteristic *types of unthinking response* to certain situations.

A human society must make for itself some design for living. It approves certain ways of meeting situations, certain ways of sizing them up. People in that society regard these solutions as *foundations of the universe.*[6]

The very deep and basic nature of these basic beliefs is brought out particularly well by Bozeman (44A), who shows that some of them go back for more than two thousand years.

As has been said in another connection, the great variety of descriptive phrases is necessary to shed light upon this concept from many sides. No person with only one point of view can explain this whole phenomenon.

We have now examined the concept of basic beliefs in general terms and are ready for a flesh-and-blood example under conditions with which we are familiar.

Our completely hypothetical example is laid in one of the restricted areas of the Pentagon where safes contain secret documents of great importance to our national security. The time is midnight. An intelligence officer who has been working late in his own office closes up his safe and is starting for home. Walking down one of the long dim corridors he meets an armed guard. They walk along together past an endless succession of deserted offices. As they pass one of the offices they are surprised to hear someone moving about. They enter and open the closed door to the inner office.

Here they are surprised to find a man who has just broken open a safe. In his pocket are found several Top Secret papers taken from the safe, including a letter from a Soviet agent offering him a large sum for the very document found on him. He is caught red-handed. There can be no question as to his guilt.

The guard says: "This scoundrel deserves to be taken out behind the Pentagon and shot right now. We could say he was shot while trying to escape. If we haul this man in and try him, what with legal delays and appeals, the proceedings will take four years and cost Uncle Sam $100,000. All this could be saved at the expense of one cartridge. He may be acquitted by pleading insanity or on some other legal technicality. His trial may disclose some facts harmful to United States security. We know he is guilty. Even if found guilty, what with one appeal after another, he will die of old age before he is executed. Why not get it over with in the next five minutes?"

At first glance the guard may seem right. There is no doubt about the guilt of the criminal. We have no sympathy for him; he is an American citizen who has turned against his friends, betrayed the trust conferred upon him as a member of the armed services, and become a traitor to the United States.

And yet—and yet we don't agree to such a summary execution. On the spur of the moment we cannot find arguments to counter the clear and cogent case presented by the guard. Yet the American readers of this book would not agree to the guard's suggestion.

Why not?

The answer lies in our deep-seated basic beliefs. We

believe that the accused has a right to be heard in his own defense. In civilization and in time of peace, we believe in a fair trial.

These are typical basic beliefs of the English-speaking world (and elsewhere). We may be slow and clumsy in supporting our beliefs with arguments. This does not worry us. *We just don't do business that way.*

The hypothetical example just described illustrates the "unthinking response." It exemplifies also some of the other descriptive phrases. It is "a deeply entrenched attitude of thought," one of "the premises on which our culture is built," and it is a part of our "social psychology." It is quite typical of this basic belief aspect of national character.[7]

This brief explanation and the example will make fairly clear the kind of beliefs that we mean, and their close association with what is more usually called traits of character. For example, the basic belief that each side in a case (and specifically the accused) has a right to be heard, is connected with the spirit of fair play. The belief that all men are created free and equal requires a spirit of tolerance.

Fundamental Philosophy of a Nation

F. S. C. Northrop has done the most to develop this concept. His book, *The Meeting of East and West, An Inquiry Concerning World Understanding* (42), gives a whole chapter to a discussion of the basic beliefs of each principal nation; and a separate section to each of many of the other nations. This book is well worth the time of any intelligence or foreign service officer, or of anyone else concerned with foreign relations. A further discussion of basic beliefs and related topics by various authors is

given in *Ideological Differences and World Order* (43).
Both of these books are classics in the field of basic
beliefs and hence of national character. The countries of
Western and Eastern Europe, Asia and Latin America are
covered, as well as the United States.

Northrop, being a philosopher, traces the philosophical
roots of many beliefs. In some cases this adds considerably
to our understanding of the situation. Of the German
people, for example, he says (42, page 213):

> It was Hegel who taught them that actual history in its
> concrete happenings, coming to fulfillment in the German
> state with its monarchical government, was not merely the
> expression of the perfect ideal, but the coming of God or
> the Absolute Spirit to self-consciousness. . . . Need one
> wonder, after such a moral and intellectual diet *taught
> throughout all their universities over a period of one hun-
> dred and fifty years,* that the German people took it easily
> and naturally for granted, not once but twice in the twen-
> tieth century that *Kultur* was by its nature and merits su-
> preme, and destined by the movement of the universe and
> the perfect moral activity of God Himself to overcome all
> opposition and embrace the world? (Emphasis is mine)

In most other cases, it seems to the present author that
Northrop overemphasizes the direct importance of the
philosophical background. His picture is more intellectual
than people really are.

Northrop (43, p. 338, as quoted by Bidney) says that
the major cultures of the Western and Eastern world
"involve basic theoretical assumptions from which the
social institutions and practices that they value proceed."
It would probably be a closer description of what
actually happens to say that there is a mutual interaction
over a long period of time between the basic theoretical

assumptions and the social institutions of a given culture. We see here another example of the Cause and/or Effect mentioned in Appendix B, whereby the basic assumptions help to mold the social institutions, and at the same time the social institutions and practices help to mold the basic assumptions.

Everyone interested in foreign relations will find it rewarding to read Northrop's vigorous, original and thought-provoking descriptions of basic beliefs and fundamental philosophy as given in *The Meeting of East and West* and *Ideological Differences and World Order* just mentioned. These ideas are further developed in a highly technical fashion, but with direct applications to national character and foreign intelligence in Northrop's *Philosophical Anthropology and Practical Politics* (43A). However, those who lack the time to read Northrop can find a simpler description of this aspect of national character in Morris' *Paths of Life* (44). His division of religions into seven types, with geometric charts showing the outstanding characteristics of each type, presents a good readable but very elementary introduction to the fundamental philosophy concept.

Difficulties in Grasping a Foreign Philosophy

It may sound tautological to say that a knowledge of the fundamental philosophy of a people is *fundamental* to an understanding of their national character, but such is the case. This aspect of a nation can never safely be ignored or even minimized in our relations with foreign countries. Unfortunately, fundamental philosophy has seldom been systematically or critically studied. Even the terms and methods of presenting it are not standard or well-understood. This situation presents difficulties in knowing and in telling. The subject itself is also inherently difficult to grasp clearly. Moreover, our society simply does not seem to turn out many top-flight philosophers or others with a desire and a talent for understanding the thought (now called ideology) of foreign peoples. This fact creates a serious problem. It is one source of the many failures of United States foreign policy in the past decade.

A further difficulty lies in the fact that such beliefs are usually below the surface; they may have no immediate clear-cut manifestations, as already mentioned.

A final difficulty arises from the fact that these fundamental premises of another people may be so different from our own that we have trouble in accepting them as real or important. At first glance they may seem absurd or childish. An intelligence officer may fall into the common error of attempting to describe and explain the basic belief of some other people in terms of his own ideas. In this case he lacks the insight into foreign thinking that an intelligence or foreign service officer should have, and he conveys a wrong impression to his readers.

As Northrop says, "the objective social scientist is the one who makes sure that the conceptualization of the facts of a foreign culture which he portrays is the conceptualization of the people in that culture rather than his own. To do this he must . . . discover their basic concepts or ideology" (45). This is one of the most difficult and also one of the most important considerations in reporting foreign intelligence so that it will convey a real understanding of a foreign people.[8]

This subject and this section are excellent illustrations of the fact that the present book cannot hope to be more than an introduction to the various aspects of national character and its practical applications.

An Example: Fundamental Philosophy in Action

How can the fundamental philosophy of a people be determined (including peoples among which we cannot carry out field investigations)? How should the results of the study be reported? How can they be used in estimating capabilities and probable courses of action?

Certainly one example is worth a thousand generalities. Fortunately such examples exist. One which serves as an excellent illustration of our present point is *The Chrysanthemum and the Sword* (41) by Ruth Benedict. As an example of what can be accomplished and of methods for attacking the problem, this is most worthy of study by any one interested in foreign relations even if he has no specific interest in Japan itself. We shall consider here primarily the first of the above questions: namely, how can the fundamental philosophy of a people be determined?

Very briefly, what is there in Benedict's point of view and methods from which an intelligence officer might profit? She was assigned to the study of Japan in June, 1944, with the mission of using the techniques of a cultural anthropologist to assist the United States to estimate the Japanese capabilities and probable courses of action in various situations connected with the conduct of war and the making of peace. She started with several serious handicaps: first, she could not visit Japan; second, she was not an expert in Japanese "area studies"; and third, shortage of time and the wartime demand for prompt conclusions.

Some of the factors which led to her outstanding success, and factors from which the Intelligence Community and Foreign Service might draw lessons, are as follows:

She already possessed broad competence and experience in her profession; namely, that of a cultural anthropologist. *Professional competence* is a solid asset to begin with. It is rarer than it should be, both in the Diplomatic Community and in the Intelligence Community.

As to the Japanese character, basic beliefs, and customs, she embarked on the project with an open mind. She was quite prepared to accept beliefs widely different from her own. This *broad-minded point of view* was a key factor in her success.

She strove to acquire a *sympathetic understanding* of the Japanese people, and, as far as it is possible for an outsider, to think like a Japanese.

Personally, or through assistants, she attacked vigorously from *every promising line of approach*, especially history, literature, mores and language, and her own previous knowledge of related Asian cultures. She interviewed Japanese living in America and Western travelers who had lived in Japan. She profited from the discussions within her own team of research workers.

In short, she pursued her researches with vigor, initiative and imagination. She really got below the surface.

What Benedict did was to construct a portrait, not of a specific Japanese, but of the way Japanese in general act. She enabled her reader to get inside the skin of a Japanese, and see the world from a very different basic viewpoint. She explained, in Japanese conceptual terms, the system of obligations which is so important in understanding any aspect of Japan.

She demonstrated the extent and intricacy of these obligations using linguistic evidence, evidence from Japan's political system, and evidence drawn from Japan's culture in its entirety. She tied these together to give a picture of the Japanese as a person who must navigate his way through a maze of obligations which often are in danger of conflicting. The depth of these obligations is seen through the behavior of the Japanese when two major obligations do in fact conflict—he discharges one of the obligations as best he can, then takes his own life to pay his now enormous debt to the obligation he has not been able to fulfill.

Benedict bases her explanation upon many levels of analysis. She shows the importance of early childhood training, of family structure, and of political organization for the portrait she develops. She depicts the Japanese in many situations, both collectively and singly. The variety of approaches she uses is itself an important control upon the objectivity of her study.

Further examples are discussed in Section 9.

NATIONAL CHARACTER
—THE CHARACTER
OF A NATION

We have discussed the meaning and make-up of character in individuals and found that in any aggregation of human beings we might expect to find individuals, very high, medium, and very low respectively in any trait of character. We have seen how the concept of individual character could be meaningfully and usefully extended to group character. We have discussed the vitally important place of organized groups (smaller than a nation) in any consideration of national character.

We have found that the concept of national character has a rational foundation and that it is now widely (although not universally) accepted by behavioral scientists and social scientists, and by some historians.

We remember again that the purpose of this whole study is *not* to train social psychologists or cultural anthropologists or to equip amateurs for field work in these disciplines. One of our purposes is to offer to the many persons interested in international relations, or directly concerned with them at any level, an opportunity to understand more deeply one fundamental aspect of international relations, namely, national character. A second purpose is to make specific, helpful contributions to the work of persons directly connected with our foreign intelligence production or with the United States Department of State, including the foreign service.

The first part of the present section covers more fully what we may mean when the word "character" is applied to a nation, and what unifying, character-forming influences are commonly nation-wide in their effect upon the individuals within a nation. Then following the subtitle on the mechanism of groups, we discuss how a characteristic group mechanism in each nation also contributes to a characteristic pattern of behavior for each nation acting as a nation.

The Character of a Nation

Nearly everything that we have learned about a group will apply also to a nation, which may be considered in general as a larger and special kind of group.

As a first approximation to a definition, we have said that *national character manifests itself as consistent patterns of national behavior* in one or more fields of activity, including fighting qualities, industry, progressive spirit, will-to-win. It arises primarily out of the character of the people as affected by their national culture. In many cases the character of the *leadership* of the controlling groups is one of the most directly influential factors.

Examples of such consistent national patterns of behavior are: the *tenacity* of the British (e.g., in continuing to fight against heavy odds in World War II); the thoroughness of the Germans (e.g., in their scholarship and in their military preparations); the optimistic, progressive spirit of the United States, with a willingness to plunge in and try anything (as shown by their settlement of the West, their industrial progress). The mechanism by which the national character of a nation becomes manifest is considered in more detail later in this section.

"All research in this field is in the last analysis directly oriented to one central type of question: What makes an Englishman an Englishman? An American an American? A Russian a Russian?" (Potter, 21)

This same central theme was voiced to me some years ago in an exasperated tone as follows: "It is sad to see that, in spite of all that the French might have learned from the English or the Americans, *the French are still as French as ever.*" De Gaulle expresses the last sentiment exactly when he says in his memoirs (45A): "How things have changed. True enough—for things, I thought. But as I looked at the noisy and excited crowd, I doubted if such was the case for the French."

Ginsberg (16) expresses the place of national character in drawing conclusions by saying that if an intelligence officer decided to draw conclusions regarding the probable future behavior of a nation which was at variance with the known behavior of this nation in the recent past, then *the burden of proof* would be on that officer to show the basis for his conclusion. For example, if one wanted to claim that modern Italy would put up a last-ditch fight in the next war, he would have to show some radically changed new conditions which would give reason to expect better long-term fighting qualities than those exhibited by the Italians in World War I or World War II.

Unifying Character-Forming Influences

Nations have many unifying character-forming influences. In any given nation, building up over a period of hundreds of years, the members share with a greater or less degree of uniformity many common elements. Some of these elements are: geographic location, climate, a common history with its triumphs and disasters, common economic interests, common political ideals, many mores and sociological factors, usually language, sometimes religion. Members of one nation often have a common literature, legends, and heroes. Usually they hold common fundamental philosophy or basic beliefs. All of this is true in spite of the many obvious exceptions.

In many countries—with Communist countries as outstanding examples—education is completely controlled by national ideology and propaganda. In all or nearly all countries, however, the national education has a marked national bias. The influence of education on individual and group beliefs and on the accepted doctrine of right and wrong is so tremendous that we would naturally expect that those subjected from childhood to the Communist education would have some aspects of character different from those who had been educated in England. Education is becoming a larger and larger part of the life of the average man nearly everywhere, and the end is not yet in sight.

A second character-forming element, the influence of which has been increasing rapidly in the past fifty years, is the *mass media*. Mass media include newspapers, magazines and books; also the movies, radio and now television. We find here again, as with education, that in the Communist countries the mass media are completely dominated by national propaganda, and that in other countries there is a more or less marked national bias. Mass media have a direct influence on those who read, hear or see them. They have an enormous total indirect influence on those who do not themselves read the newspaper or hear the radio, but who talk with those who do. Again we expect that such a powerful influence, differing so much from nation to nation, would help to produce corresponding differences directly in individual character and secondarily in national character from nation to nation.

Mass media are examples of the Vice Versa effect mentioned in Appendix B. Mass media influence the national character, but mass media also *reflect* the national character and are influenced by it. This is a typical instance of "reciprocal interaction." The British Royal Commission on the Press (1949) suggested that the more massive the media, the less it molds and the more it reflects. This statement is probably much more true in the Free World than in the U.S.S.R. However, even the Soviets have admitted that their massive propaganda has occasionally produced not conviction, but boredom.

With so many character-forming elements in common, it is natural to expect that many of the members of a nation would develop a certain similarity in their basic beliefs, points of view, sources of inspiration or taboo, and other factors—in fact in their character. Thus it would be expected that the nation as a whole would develop patterns of behavior which its nationals would adopt with a considerable degree of uniformity as evidences of its national character.

For the valuable and pertinent contributions of philosophical anthropology to this subject see Northrop (43A), Chapter 5, "What Is a Nation?"

Furthermore, habits and customs in a people which are usually found to be successful—that is, to produce desirable results—often come to be regarded as morally "right," and the unsuccessful customs as morally "wrong." Common ideas of right and wrong are certainly productive of a common character in the members of a group or nation.

Most nations have experienced in the past numerous changes in their national boundaries, although as a rule a nation has remained in the same general part of the world with little change in the location of its cultural center. This would be true, for example, of England, France, Spain, Italy, Greece, China, Japan, Russia proper (with some reservations), Germany (with reservations).

We know that the action of a given nation in a given situation is the net result of many interrelated factors, just as is the case of an individual. We know that the nationals within a country are not unanimous; those favoring the action taken by the nation may even be a small minority, in some cases a small governing class. Nevertheless most nations, like most individuals, do have a characteristic pattern of behavior. This is sufficiently consistent to make it a highly useful factor in estimating probable courses of action or other considerations pertaining to that nation.

But the national character is not the arithmetic mean of the character of the individuals in the nation, any more than the football-playing ability of a football team could be computed by considering the average weight, running ability, passing ability, kicking ability of the members of the team.

In the Nine Principles of Intelligence described in my book, *Strategic Intelligence Production* (38), I include national character as one of these principles under the name of "the spirit of the people." This term has a special value in that it suggests as a part of national character the inclusion of the emotional and spiritual elements which are important factors in all human activities.

In an important crisis, national action arising in part out of national character is more than mechanical behavior which could be carried out by a machine. It is more than the coldly calculated behavior activated by pure reason, which could conceivably emerge from a computer or electronic brain (falsely named). The national action includes also some warm human emotions such as love or hate, patriotism or short-sighted selfishness, optimism or cynicism, hope or fear.

The human emotions, with all of their unpredictabilities, are a vital part of the intelligence picture, and are especially evident when character is considered. The intelligence officer who forgets this, is of the type who can see no important difference between a well-stuffed eagle and a live bird.

Personal character changes with time. The reckless youth may become the cautious man of middle age. Such changes are slow and do not affect ordinary personal dealings. In much the same way the character of a nation normally changes somewhat from century to century. Such change is an example of the universal rule that all human institutions change with time. However, until recently most changes in national character have been so slow that they did not affect the current intelligence estimates or the given international situation. Since World War I the changes in the character of some nations have been much more rapid. This is discussed in Section 12. A practical point is that in judging the character of a nation, the character which it exhibited several centuries ago may or may not be pertinent.

The Mechanism [1] by Which Groups Affect Character

We now come to the character of a nation acting as such. By nation we mean a large group under one sovereign government having its own foreign relations and usually possessing also common territorial and language bonds. This is the unit sometimes referred to as a "state" and sometimes as a "nation-state." Sorokin (25, p. 254) says: "We have seen that each of these bonds—the territorial, the state, and the language bond—

exerts a tangible influence upon the physical, mental, moral, and behavioral characteristics of the members of the group and upon their organization and culture. When all three are compounded, they exert a still stronger effect. In their totality they produce a 'national type.'"
Under modern conditions nations are evidently the most powerful and important large groups. This is largely due to their authority over their own members, and to their sovereign power in dealing with other nations.

For one of the most interesting and worthwhile discussions of this topic see Deutsch (46), who discusses also character-forming agencies.

We have seen that it is meaningful and useful to speak of national character in the meaning of the character of the nation acting as such. A nation can be said to be progressive or backward, aggressive or friendly (a good neighbor), warlike or peaceful, and so on. From what roots do these traits of national character (still meaning the character of the nation acting as a nation) arise? [2]

To a considerable extent they may arise directly from the character of the individuals within the nation acting individually directly on the nation, rather than through any group. For example in a nation like the United States, a large number of farmers, each making his own free, individual choice may decide to buy tractors; and a large number of manufacturers may decide to purchase modern machinery. Similar free choices are made by other United States citizens in regard to modern methods of banking and education. All of these individual progressive choices are influenced by the progressive character of the individuals, and would lead directly to the United States acquiring a progressive national character without the intervention of groups. In the same period of time, the members of some other nation having more conservative individual characters might individually usually decide one after the other to stick to horses on the farm, to the old machinery, to old banking, and dated forms of education. The character of such a nation would become more and more backward.

On the other hand, traits of character of the nation acting as such may be transmitted to the nation through the medium of the groups within the nation instead of directly through individuals. Beard (47) is correct when he says: "This great fact stands out clearly, that through the centuries—down until our own day—group interests were recognized as forming the very essence of politics both in theory and practice."

The *mechanism* by which organized groups, often acting as pressure groups, make their character and wishes felt politically is one of the central themes of political science as described in the quotations herein from Lasswell and Kaplan (27). See also Burns and Peltason (48). It is true that millions of individuals who feel definitely but mildly on a certain subject do not have as much practical effect as a few thousand who feel strongly enough on the subject to put up an organized political fight as a group. It is the organized pressure groups which have an effect on national character out of all proportion to their size. It is they who often bring about the phenomenon whereby, even in a democracy, an organized minority can impose its will on a majority. (For example, in the United States today, the farmers with their ever-increasing billions in surpluses.) Pressure groups can often achieve positive ends. Even more often, and much more easily, they can *prevent* action being taken to which they are opposed.[3]

In considering the effects of personal, group, and national character on a given situation, the number of factors which may exert *some* influence—large or small, direct or indirect—on the final outcome is enormous. To make practical applications of the concept of character to practical problems, it is always necessary to simplify the problem before us by concentrating our attention on the most important factors. We thus arrive at a "first approximation" which may or may not be modified by deeper studies.

For the purpose of such simplification in starting to estimate the effect of groups on national character or national action, it is often helpful to consider which are the dominant groups in a given problem. This is what the practical politician does every day, consciously or unconsciously. Groups which are dominant in one situation may exert little influence in another. Thus in the United States the Jewish vote as a unified group must be reckoned with in some questions of foreign policy, but not in others. In the United States the trade unions and farmers are usually found among the dominant groups. In this country—contrary to some other nations—the Army and the Communists are fortunately not dominant groups, and do not normally strongly influence our national character.

Political Parties and National Character

As an example of the critical importance which group action may have, in contrast to individual action, let us consider simplified and idealized versions of two nations somewhat resembling France and England respectively. Suppose that for the sake of this illustration the distribution of voting individuals as between conservatives and radicals (rightists and leftists) is exactly the same. Suppose for example that in each nation 5 per cent are rigid reactionaries, and 5 per cent are the most aggressive kind of Communists, and suppose that the gradations in between as to degree of conservatism or radicalism are just the same in the two nations.

Now suppose that this continuous spectrum of individuals from right to left, as in France, divides itself into about seven major political parties or factions. No party can ever have anything near a majority. The only way in which any ministry can obtain a majority is by building up some sort of a precarious coalition of parties which *have no loyalty to one another*. Under this setup of political groups, politicians spend most of their time in plots and counterplots. There is little chance for the implementation of any long-range constructive policy. The coalition has no stability. Ministries come and go with the resulting inefficiency and disunity which we have witnessed in France for so many years.[4]

Now let us assume, as a contrast, that individuals representing exactly the same shades of political opinion from right to left in the same proportions and in the same intensities, were willing to divide themselves into *two* political parties instead of seven. Suppose that the larger part of each of these parties held together through victory and defeat; each party enforced discipline within the party, and built up a tradition of loyalty to the party among its members. A shift of a small percentage of the voters from one party to the other would then be sufficient to bring about a change in the administration. Yet each of the major parties would hold together as a responsible organization hoping to deserve the public confidence.

Then we would have the *two*-party system similar to that of England and America.[5] This is humorously but nonetheless effectively described in the Gilbert and Sullivan opera *Iolanthe* in the words of Private Willis:

I often think it's comical
How Nature always does contrive
That every boy and every gal
    That's born into the world alive
Is either a little Liberal
    Or else a little Conservative!

When individuals with the same shades of political opinion are willing to divide into two more or less permanent and responsible major political parties (or groups) instead of six or seven, it makes all the difference as to the accomplishments of the nation.

Please note that a rather extensive field test of the character of individuals within these two contrasting countries might find no significant difference between them, if the test concentrated on the conservatism versus radicalism, or on many other objectives (political, economic, educational, for example). These and many other traits of character might well be exactly the same in the two countries in distribution of opinion and in intensity. When the tests are confined to individual character, this essential difference between the two nations would only be detected if the questions asked were skilful enough to bring out those traits of character upon which depends the ability to co-operate consistently in two major political parties. However, *when groups are considered* in addition to individuals, then this essential factor in national character immediately stands out.

Individuals and Groups within the Nation

In summary, when we are interested in the capabilities and probable courses of action of a given nation in those fields of action where the nation acts officially as a nation, one factor to consider is always the national character of the *nation as such*. National character in this sense is affected in part by individual character. Here we must consider not only the numbers but the intensity of their feeling. Public opinion polls that omit the intensity factor neglect an essential part of the picture.

Where there is little unity in the nation as a whole, it may be better, and it is certainly more logical, first to give consideration to the character of the major influential groups within the nation, and then to consider how these groups, acting within the national mechanism, will affect the over-all action of the nation as a whole. Such competing groups to be selected for early consideration may be geographical (as was once the case with England and Scotland in the United Kingdom); or they may be religious, as was the case in what was formerly India; or by language, or otherwise.

So group character is found to be important from many angles. Individuals who feel intensely usually organize themselves into active groups. An intelligence officer or anyone else who is interested in the capabilities and probable courses of action of a nation would do well to study the character of the active groups and the mechanism of their political action as a background for his estimation.

National Character as a Vital Factor in Each Component

Of the principal elements affecting international relations, which are also the recognized components of strategic intelligence, those in which national character plays a vital role are:

Military
Economic

Political
Scientific
Sociological
Geographical
Transportation and Communications
Biographical

An intelligence estimate regarding a given nation usually covers that nation's capabilities in regard to at least one or sometimes all of these components and then its "probable courses of action" under certain circumstances. Much of this could be summed up by the words "developments to be expected from the given nation in the foreseeable future."

Right away we see that developments to be expected always involve at least two major kinds of factors (plus others in special circumstances). One factor is *hard facts*. The other is the *character of the people* who utilize these facts, either directly or through their government.

A brief consideration of three of the above mentioned components will illustrate the present point, and indicate how it may be applied to any or all of the components.

1. *Military strength.* The two major factors are: *hard facts* regarding weapons, ammunition, size and training of the armed forces, all as affected by *national character* as evidenced by courage, patriotism, national unity in a crisis, tenacity, will-to-win, and other traits of character. Briefly: *weapons* x *character of people* using the weapons. For examples of national character as a decisive factor when considering military strength, compare (a) the fighting quality of the French army at the outbreak of World War II with (b) the fighting qualities of the German army at that period. On the basis of statistics the French army was the strongest in Europe. Its fatal weaknesses were not derived from the hard facts, such

as numbers of soldiers and weapons, but from intangible factors, including the character of their leaders and of the French nation.

In military strength history shows repeatedly that the character of the people has produced results *just the opposite* of what would reasonably have been expected from the usual Army Staff College thinking, if based only upon quantities of soldiers and munitions. For a most readable account, see "On Relative Strengths" by Akram (50A). See also Knorr (50B), who says: "Physical munitions provide ability to fight. Motivation provides the will to fight."

2. *Economics and industry.* Here again there are at least two primary factors: (a) *Hard facts* of economic facilities—mineral deposits, farms, water power, factories and harbors—all as affected by (b) *National character*, as evidenced by industry, progressiveness, optimism, will-to-win. For an example of the vital influence of the character of the people who exploit the mineral deposits, plough the fields, or implement the national industrial expansion, compare French with German industry from 1870 to 1914. Or compare Mexican industrial conditions with those in the U.S. just over the border in California and Texas, where the natural resources are essentially the same. Briefly: *natural resources* x *character of the people* exploiting the resources.

This simple expression, *hard facts* x *national character*, provides an important part of what we need to know in estimating the outcome of a given situation. It is useful because it brings out clearly that hard physical facts seldom have much operational significance in human affairs *unless considered in connection with the character of the people* and the groups who will use these weapons, natural resources, and so forth as the case may be. To make the expression clear and meaningful, the character should be stated in terms of the pertinent traits of character which are *favorable* to the use of the hard facts under consideration.

Thus in the use of weapons, one factor would express the degree of courage under any convenient convention. Ordinary fighting quality could be expressed as 1. Better and better fighting qualities by 2, 3, 4, and so on up to 10 as the "do or die." Then low fighting qualities by fractions, 0.9 signifying a little below average. This fraction could evidently go down to 0.1, and certainly to zero. Some men have no combat capabilities with any weapon under any circumstances.

Similarly, when considering natural resources *industry* would be expressed by positive integers. Laziness by fractions.

In my earlier discussion of "the spirit of the people" as one of the nine principles of intelligence (38), I sum this up by saying: "An unusually aggressive spirit on the one hand or a defeatist spirit on the other hand may multiply the capability which would ordinarily be expected from a given situation by ten or one tenth respectively."

So we have here a simple statement which helps us to understand and to remember the interrelation of two or three highly important factors, and which can guide our judgment in estimating the probable outcome of many situations. It would be a mistake to think that this expression has the precision of mathematics. In theory an equation for a numerical value of the achievement to be expected in a given situation could be built up by assigning "weights" to many elements of the situation. Such a process would give a misleading appearance of precision and certainty. Such an elaboration of this simple but useful concept would not be justified for the purpose of the present sutdy.

Like many other methods for attacking problems in the

area of foreign intelligence and foreign affairs, it is better to regard this concept as supplying a useful *guide to our judgment* rather than as attempting to supply the final answer.

3. *Political.* It has been pointed out by Spalding (51) that, when critically examined, the British Constitution is on the face of it one of the most inefficient constitutions in Europe or America. Yet it has worked outstandingly well as compared with other European and American constitutions over the past 150 years and longer. The *hard facts* [6] of the British Constitution (as established largely by custom and in part by such statutes as the Bill of Rights) demonstrate its weaknesses and absurdities. It works outstandingly well because of the national character of those who make it work.[7] It has continued to work in peace and in war, in periods of great prosperity and in long, lean periods of near bankruptcy for the same reason. The best strategic intelligence forecast is that which will continue to work well beyond the lifetime of those now living.

As another example, one of the most amusing articles in *Punch* in 1958 described an imaginary British infantry battalion returning from summer maneuvers. On approaching London, the commanding officer suddenly decides to march into the city and *take over control of the British Government*—which he did without difficulty. As an intelligence paper discussing "capabilities" according to our highest current standards, this paper is beyond criticism. Tested by war gaming, its conclusions are sound. And yet it is absurd and amusing for only one little intangible reason which is at variance with all the hard facts of military strength—namely, the British national character.

One more example. During the debates over a single Department of Defense in the United States many in Congress voiced the fear of a military dictatorship. It was pointed out, however, that in many Latin American countries, where the law was most emphatic as to civilian control, military coups were the most common. It was almost timidly suggested that perhaps the national character of the United States *must* be considered when deciding on the dangers of a strong Department of Defense.

For similar reasons I can state that the military capabilities of the Armed Forces actually working in the Pentagon are not a threat to the defenseless senators and congressmen in the Capitol and nearby office buildings. Based on fire power I am wrong; but the national character of the United States is such that we don't do business that way.

Similarly for the scientific, sociological, geographical, communication and biographical components of strategic intelligence—national character raises its head again and again *as a decisive factor which cannot safely be overlooked.*

For Completeness Three Factors—Each Different in Kind

This concept, using two major factors, namely, *hard facts* x *national character,* to estimate the capabilities and probable courses of action of a given *nation* (say Poland) in a given *activity* (say some phase of economics such as agriculture), has convenience and great practical value. To round this out we should add a third factor to represent the *situation* in which this activity would be carried out (starting with the present situation) and looking ahead for the period of the estimate.[8] As in the case of the other two factors, the elements of the situation *favorable* to the activity in question are expressed as positive integers. Unfavorable elements are expressed as fractions with zero as the limit, when the situation renders the activity impossible.

For example, in estimating the capabilities and probable development in certain agricultural production (e.g., wheat) to be expected in Poland within the next three years, we would then consider:

HF x NC x Sit

The HF being the hard facts pertaining to recent and present wheat production such as soil, climate, acreage suitable for wheat, and agricultural equipment.

NC being the national character of the Polish people who are to provide the means, and are to plant and harvest the wheat. Are they hard-working, progressive in farming methods? Is there sufficient unity and a will-to-win?

Sit being the other important and pertinent elements of the situation. This is admittedly a catch-all. To retain our concentration on the essentials, Sit must be restricted to the few most important pertinent factors in the background situation. In some cases, however, the situation is crucial. For example, a warlike people with good weapons might fight well in a popular war, but poorly in an unpopular war.

This concept of the *three* major factors is psychologically effective because each of the three factors is of a different sort; each requires a different kind of analyst to supply and interpret that factor. It thus has the broad base necessary to give reliable foundations for sound conclusions. So data for each factor may preferably come initially from a different kind of person, even from a different department of the government. For example, hard facts are definite and invite precision. Furthermore, the real meaning of most hard facts is best obtained from an expert in that field. Thus military facts can best be inter-

preted by a military man; agricultural facts by an agricul-
turalist; and so on. On the other hand, national character
is a matter of understanding and mature judgment. The
most reliable judgment of the character of Poland and
the Poles must come from some one who has lived there,
has studied there, and become something of an area
specialist.

The concept of three factors makes sure that all three
are duly considered. It is logical and is economical of
time and mental effort. It brings out the *necessity for
teamwork* in foreign intelligence or in understanding
foreign affairs in accordance with the basic purpose of
this book. It is a constant reminder that national character
can never be omitted in the understanding, estimating,
planning, or practice of international relations. So to sum
up this practical suggestion we repeat:

HF x NC x Sit = *estimate of the probable outcome.*

Practical Method for Estimating Group Character

We have shown that in foreign intelligence and foreign
relations it is often tremendously important to estimate
what some group can and will in fact do in a given situation. To make such an estimate we must make a careful
study of the situation before us. The terms of reference
of such a study must be stated as clearly and specifically
as possible. As examples:

1. At a given time and place with a given combat
mission, what will a given infantry company probably
accomplish?

2. In a given present or near-future political campaign
with known issues, what will a given political party (e.g.,
the British Labor Party) probably accomplish?

3. In the case of a threatened strike by a given labor
union at a given time and place and under given circum-

stances, what action will the union probably take and what success will it probably have in accomplishing its objectives?

We have seen above that the outcome of the action of a group or nation can often be estimated by the product of three factors: *hard facts* x *character* x *situation.* In the simplest example just given, namely the infantry company, the Hard Facts would include weapons, ammunition, training, etc. The Situation would include terrain, weather, obstacles, enemy opposition, etc. The purpose of the present discussion is to examine methods for estimating group character which would be pertinent to the given situation and which would thus provide us with one of the three vital factors in making our estimate of the outcome.

We are now therefore looking for practical methods for estimating group character which can be carried out with some success by the means at hand, and which will enable us to get results in time to be of service. Results can never be certain; but they can give us knowledge and understanding of the problem before us which will be specifically helpful and worth the effort involved.

In theory almost every trait of character enters to some extent, however small, into the character of the group as a whole. In theory we should perhaps make a thorough psychological and psychoanalytical examination of every member. However, the purpose of this discussion is to develop methods which will be *practically useful.* This makes it necessary to eliminate nonessentials, to make a wise selection of the important elements, and then to concentrate our attention on these key elements.

We suggest that the following selection of important elements, workable methods, and useful approaches will be practical for estimating group character under a great variety of conditions.

Expedient A

First, as to the traits of character to be considered, in any given situation we can focus on the few which are of outstanding importance in that situation and normally give only brief consideration to the others. For example, physical courage is of first importance for the infantryman, but of no importance to a political party member.

Expedient B

As a simplifying concept which presents the facts correctly and usefully as far as it pretends to go, we introduce the term "effective character" of a group or part of a group. This effective character comprises the traits of character which must have been prominent in the group as a whole to lead it to accomplish what it actually did accomplish in view of the advantages which it had and the difficulties which it faced.

As an example take the pioneers in North America, 1700 to 1850, who pushed back from the Atlantic coast and established settlements. They did actually rapidly push westward in spite of many dangers and hardships. They did actually hold on to the land they had cleared, improve their settlements, establish self-government, and continue the westward movement. Admitting that there were a considerable number of such pioneers who were lazy, timid, unprogressive and dishonest, it is fair to say that the *effective character* of the pioneer group as a whole was vigorous, courageous, tenacious, progressive and liberal.

The concept of the effective character does not necessarily imply that this character is possessed by the leaders, or by a majority of the members, or that it is the "modal personality or character" (a term beloved by some social psychologists [9]). For example, it has been clearly demonstrated by field studies that toward the end of World War II the presence of only two dedicated Nazis in a platoon of, say, thirty German soldiers was sufficient to maintain a tenacious and courageous effective character for the platoon as shown by stubborn fighting qualities, even when the great majority of the other soldiers considered the situation hopeless and wished to surrender. Again the effective character of the British people in 1940 was courageous and vigorous, whereas their leader, Chamberlain, did not possess that type of character.

The effective character of a group is indicated by the character associated with the *net results of the action of the group* as a whole. It does not in itself tell us the inner workings by which this result was achieved.

Expedient C

For the purpose of making practical applications of group character we make the simplifying assumption that we can obtain a satisfactory working knowledge of most groups which have any real unity of purpose and character by dividing our study of the character of the group into three categories: The leadership; the mass of the members; the dissatisfied, perhaps radical or suppressed minority (if any).

The leaders are few and prominent. The nature of their leadership is in general knowable. We can often know much about the personal characters of leaders even in hostile countries. The mass of the membership generally has an effective character which is knowable. The degree to which it can or should profitably be broken down into parts for a study will depend upon the circumstances. Finally the dissatisfied minority (if any) may be an active and vocal opposition to the present group leadership, or it may be hidden. It may be active undercover, or sullenly and secretly hostile. It may consist of a few cranks, or it may comprise the leaders of tomorrow. Its aims and character are worth knowing where possible. It is the most difficult of the three categories in a group for a foreigner to get to know.

The dissenting minority may now be so small or so submerged that it is overlooked or underestimated; yet it may be of the greatest importance to the intelligence officer or foreign service officer. Recent international events have given only too many examples of the folly of neglecting to consider dissident minorities.

The subject of the dissenting minority is presented with striking insight in the *True Believer* by Eric Hoffer (51B), and analytically and fruitfully by Deutsch (46).

To sum up: In estimating the character of a given group in a given situation the following methods are often helpful:

a) Concentrate on those traits of character pertinent to the situation.
b) The concept of the "effective character" of a group or a part of a group may be fruitful.
c) Consider separately the characters of the leaders, the central mass of the members, and the dissenting minority. The last may be of unsuspected importance.

The Long Pull vs. the Short Pull

It is important to note that in regard to a nation's capabilities and probable courses of action in a given activity, its national character often has more effect on the results of the long pull than of the short pull. National character is more important as a factor in a nation's final achievements than in what it starts.

The *beginning* of a new national activity may depend upon a wave of superficial enthusiasm, or take place because a nation is forced into the action by unexpected developments, or it may occur by pure chance. Compared with the needs of the long pull, it takes very little ability in any direction to declare war, or to found a colony, or to take the first step toward industrialization (or *toward* anything else). It is in the conduct of the war, or in the management of the colonies, or in the initiative and energy to make industrialization successful that we see the effect of traits of national character stand out most clearly.

The day-to-day fighting in warfare, or the day-after-day efforts of the early colonists, or the continued industrial struggle brings out the best or the worst in all three echelons of national character; namely, the character of individuals; the character of the groups which are directly concerned with the activity in question; and finally the character of the nation or people as a whole and acting as a nation, in co-ordinating its resources to prosecute the war vigorously and courageously; or to support the colonies in adversity and govern them wisely; or to give wise and imaginative support to new industries.

The Key to the German Defeats

British character is the subject of a book of fiction entitled *The Sixth Column* (51C). Although the subject is given a humorous treatment in that book, it contains elements of truth, and it makes clear the point of view which I am presenting here. The book describes a hypothetical conference of Germans shortly after World War II. The Germans felt that they had started two world wars with better plans and better arms than their opponents. The German armies were much better fighting organizations than the armies on the other side. Germany was better prepared in every way. Yet they were twice defeated. What was the basic cause of their defeat? How could they do better next time?

After a careful and systematic study, they came to the conclusion that *the one factor* which was the fundamental cause of their two defeats and which if different would have resulted in a German victory in each war was the British national character.

In World War I the British did not have to enter the war at all. Many people thought they would not do so. They had at the outset "a contemptible little army." They suffered enormous casualties and had apparently very little to gain. But for some reason they *did* enter the war, and they *did* stick it out in the face of increasing discouragement till they reached a victorious conclusion, contrary to what anyone had a right to expect.

In World War II the story was quite similar except that for a crucial period the British were the *only* people which continued the struggle against the Germans. Again they unreasonably persisted, in spite of a long series of defeats by land and by sea.

The answer to the Germans' original question was evident: It was not arms or industrial strength or diplomacy which was responsible for their defeats; it was simply the British character. Likewise, the solution of the German problem as to how to win the next war was equally evident. They had only to change the British character! This the Germans then proceeded to attempt with the most modern and approved techniques of mass advertising, propaganda, and psychological warfare, doubtless drawing upon the German equivalent of Madison Avenue for advertising talent.

The germ of truth contained herein makes this bit of fiction worth recounting.

THE SPIRIT OF YOUTH
AND ITS OPPOSITE

Categories are often useful in discussing human problems—provided one does not take them too seriously. So in considering the character of nations, it is often convenient and useful to describe some nations as having the spirit of youth and others as having the spirit of old age.

First, let me invite attention to what I mean. I do not mean that the nations in the first category are *chronologically* young. That description has little definite meaning. It all depends upon the date from which you decide to start counting. It is evident that the use of these two categories—youth and old age—carries echoes of Toynbee, but without Toynbee's broad claims as to civilizations and cycles. In the present book there is no implication that a given nation normally or permanently proceeds chronologically from a time of youth, through a time of maturity, to a time of old age.

In fact, we find certain nations which have experienced a number of fairly well-marked fluctuations in their youthful spirit. In the given nation a period of youthfulness has often been followed by a period of full flowering maturity, then a period of static conditions or of decline. Some rejuvenating idea or situation may then occur, which opens up great new possibilities and leads to a new wave, including the period of youth and expansion, the period of mature flowering and the decline. The declines here mentioned are usually not complete disintegration and death like the fall of the Roman Empire. They certainly involve a temporary end of the youthful spirit and of the distinct "golden age." The modern word for such a decline is "recession." This is here applied to the mental and spiritual aspects of life as well as to the economic and military aspects.

In general the youthful period is the time of vigorous striving. This grades into the mature period in which the fruits are reaped and enjoyed. The mature periods represent the "golden ages" and are therefore the most spectacular and the best known. The youthful periods of striving before the golden rewards are obtained are sometimes overlooked or forgotten.

Some examples of this youthful spirit are: For Rome the period of the Carthaginian Wars; for Greece the period of the Persian Wars to be followed by the mature Age of Pericles, and the ensuing decline after the Peloponnesian Wars. In the United States certainly the nineteenth century; for Germany a period characterized by a youthful spirit began about 1848 and merged into the remarkable flowering of German nationalism from the 1870's till 1914. This full flowering showed itself by outstanding achievements militarily, industrially, scientifically, and in other intellectual fields. For England the Elizabethan period, and probably also the period of industrial and territorial expansion and intellectual flowering called Victorian.

A motley crew, you may say. What can they possibly

have in common? What useful purpose can such a category serve?

At the other end of the scale and as typical examples of nations showing a spirit of old age, let us merely cite: Italy in the eighteenth century; France, 1920 to 1958; and Egypt in the fifteenth through the eighteenth centuries; although there are plenty of others in this category.

These two categories are useful because of the boundlessness of the field in which studies of foreign relations must operate. In this field almost anything is possible. If he had infinite time, the student of foreign relations could investigate every possibility. However, as his time is always limited, any device which helps him to *focus attention on the few most promising lines of attack* is tremendously valuable. In fact, a constant selection of some facts and elimination of others *must* be made at every turn of an investigation in this field. Being thus guided, the intelligence officer or student of foreign affairs is more likely to spend his efforts where the rewards are greatest.

So the usefulness of a consideration of the category of the Spirit of Youth lies in the fact that in nations having such a spirit we often find a certain *package of traits* of *character* and certain typical situations. If the intelligence officer believes that a foreign country comes in this category he will *expect* to find all or most of the traits listed below. He cannot *assume* that they are present. He must look for them. However, it usually saves time to know what to look for.

The Institute for International Social Research at Princeton has developed a "Striving Scale" as a means of studying at least one facet of national character and self-appraisal. In using this device each individual under study is asked to regard life as a ladder with ten rungs. The top rung represents the mode of life which the individual would consider most desirable and the bottom rung the one which he would consider least desirable, with the other degrees of desirability represented by the rungs in between. He is then asked to state on which rung he considers that he now stands, and on which rung he believes he has a chance to be in the future.

This simple interviewing device gives promise of great usefulness in many forms of social research. Any method which throws light on individual character can be used also in a study of group or national character. Interesting comparative studies can be made between groups, or on the same group at different periods of its existence. It would be pertinent to the study of the spirit of youth and of old age in a nation.

The Spirit of Youth

Nations possessed of the spirit of youth usually have most of the following traits of character: optimism, enthusiasm, a progressive spirit, often an aggressive spirit and the will-to-win. Parts of the economy are often expanding; the birth rate is high. There is an outburst of nationalism and patriotic pride. This is often shown in literature. Sometimes in art or scholarship. In short, it is for that nation an age of progress. They believe figuratively in an expanding universe, although it is not necessarily a time of military conquests.

The Spirit of Old Age

By contrast the nation overshadowed by the spirit of old age has in general the opposite of these traits of character just mentioned. This results in pessimism, passive resignation, resistance to change or to new ideas; a defensive spirit. The economy may be static or shrinking and the birth rate low. One characteristic not quite so evident at first glance is a cynicism and spirit of disillusionment. This is first seen in politics. The plans of their own statesmen for improvement are greeted with cynicism. Most of the people regard all politicians as charlatans. There are no living national heroes. It is hard to arouse such people to any concerted effort to better themselves. In politics, ministries fall at short intervals. Both government and business are inefficient and corrupt. Sometimes such a character paves the way for military or economic defeats. Sometimes it leads to a dictatorship.[1]

It has been said that a nation which has passed through the spirit of youth and is now in the grip of the spirit of old age can understand the feelings and attitudes of other nations still in the youthful stage because the first nation has itself passed through this stage and so "remembers" its own youth from actual memory or from its own history. However, so it is said, a new youthful nation has difficulty in understanding or sympathizing with a nation in the old age category if the youthful nation has never had the old-age experience. If true, this would explain the difficulty which most Americans have in understanding the character of modern Spain or Italy, for example.

Not all nations, of course, during any given period of study fit typically into either of these two categories, and so cannot be usefully studied from this point of view. Some do.

These two categories have been applied to groups as well as to nations, but using different terms (27). As groups become more mature and lose the impetuosity of youth, "the *agitational* phase of social action moves into the *organizational; ideology* becomes *phraseology;* the *prophet* becomes the *tactician;* the *enthusiast* becomes the *bureaucrat.*"

Evidently the concept of these two interesting categories of character can be expanded as much as desired by an exploration of its capabilities and limitations; by historical examples and exceptions, which latter may be the more fruitful for study.

SOURCES OF INFORMATION
ON THE CHARACTERS OF
SPECIFIC NATIONS

Where can a person interested in the various aspects of international relations find specific information on national character in a given case?

It is true that the files of United States government departments and of any large library are filled with books, articles and other documents pertaining to the history, geography, exports, imports, population and other facts about nearly all foreign countries. Publications on the subjects dealing with such facts are easy to recognize by their titles, and are usually easy to evaluate. But how can one find similar material on national character?

In the first place let us see what we really want. Pertinent preliminary questions are: Who do we consider that "we" are, and what are our purposes in digging into questions of national character?

In this case "we" may be, as mentioned in the preface, foreign intelligence officers, or foreign service officers, or officers of the armed services, or members of one of the many United States government departments or agencies concerned with foreign relations; or we may be members of educational or research institutions concerned with political science, sociology, anthropology, social psychology or any of the international aspects of the other social sciences or the humanities; or we may be intelligent members of the general public with an enlightened interest in international affairs.

The purpose of each of us is to gain that knowledge and understanding which will help each of us to carry out his own mission better than he could without this consideration of national character.

By contrast, "we" are *not* concerned in this book with advancing the theoretical principles upon which the social sciences are based (valuable as this is). We are, however, much concerned with the *applications* of the somewhat imperfect knowledge of national character which is available right now to the present and near-future problems of foreign intelligence and international relations.

An intelligence officer, or foreign service officer, or other person concerned, does not have to be a historian or a geographer in order to make intelligent use of history and geography in his duties. In exactly the same way this officer should be able to select, to understand and to use wisely the studies on national character which specialists in this field have already prepared without trying to become either a psychologist or an anthropologist. Rewarding results depend most of all upon his initiative and *desire to gain as full as possible an understanding of the character of the people concerned.*

What Kind of People Are They?

In setting out to gain a knowledge of the national character of any country we must always start by building up our own general background of knowledge of that country, if such a background does not already exist. This should be just as comprehensive as the importance of the problem, the time, and the information available permit. For any country it should always include, of course, its history, geography, weather, language, economics, political organizations and conditions, sociology, including education and religion and population, personalities, military situation, etc. All these in their broadest aspects. Special attention should be given to recent and impending changes. All of this background is *essential*. I say little more about it here because this book starts from where the usual studies of history, economics and geography stop.

Having this background, we are now ready to consider national character specifically. We might put this stage of the problem as follows: For a given people, after we have digested all of the usual pertinent facts and statistics, and understood their institutions and general way of living—then *what kind of people are they?* How do they think, believe and act? Considering the pertinent traits of personal character noted in Section 4, to what extent is each trait found to a high, medium, or low degree in the important groups of the population? Considering the nation acting as a nation in its relations with other nations, what traits of character would we expect the nation as a whole to exhibit, such as honesty, reliability, co-operativeness (a good-neighbor policy), industry, tenacity, aggressiveness, will-to-win, progressiveness, optimism, etc.? What are the nation's basic beliefs, outstanding loyalties, taboos, aspirations and fears? What picture does the nation have of itself in relation to other peoples?

Titles of Publications

In some cases published studies which include the national character of a nation or a people, or of a smaller group, bear the word "character" in the title or the subtitle. As to subtitles, see for example *The Lonely Crowd, A Study of the Changing American Character* by Riesman, *et al.* (12). Often it is evident that a consideration of character is included in a study even when another term is used in the title, as in Lerner's *America as a Civilization* (52). Sometimes "personality" or "mind" or "style" are used in a title as more or less synonymous with "character." Often a book or article contains material pertinent to the study of character when it discusses culture and occasionally when it discusses values or ideology.

When going over titles in the search for publications containing material which will help us to gain an understanding of the character of a foreign people, the criterion is: Is a part of this publication largely concerned with what kind of people these are and what they think, and believe and value? If so, this will probably help us. An example is Middleton's *These Are the British* (53).

It is perfectly evident from his title that he is trying to tell us the kind of people that the British are. However, if the author's main concern is with facts, or statistics of any kind, or with economics, organization charts, etc., then he probably has little or nothing bearing directly on national character. His contribution, if any, to our problem would lie in showing the mechanism by which a nation is caused to act through the activities of certain of its parties, groups or elites.

An ambitious collection of descriptions of peoples and nations, often including their character, was made during World War II (53A). These vary in quality. Some parts of the projects which are included under modern "area studies" at various universities and other research institutions may also be very valuable.

An excellent example of the kind of study that gives us exactly what we are looking for in our effort to understand national character "at a distance" is the section on Greece in the chapter, "Studies of Whole Cultures" in Mead's book on *Cultural Patterns and Technical Change* (53B). In about forty closely packed pages there is hardly a statistic. Nothing is quantified. It is just a description of what kind of people the Greeks are and how they think, feel and react. Much of their behavior following World War II could have been foretold from such a study of this "whole culture." The description was written from the firsthand knowledge of one who was born and raised in Greece, supplemented by written material and interviews.

Unprofitable Approaches

As far as the practical applications of national character to foreign intelligence or international relations are concerned, as discussed in this book, little or no benefits will be derived from direct use of the concepts of the "oral, anal and genital" types of personality. Little or nothing *for our purposes* is gained by direct applications of the infant feeding and the "toilet seat" school of psychology. Similarly, approaches to our problems using the concepts and terminology of the psychiatrist and the psychoanalyst are not yet sufficiently well-founded to warrant practical use here. All of these concepts are useful in basic research into the principles of psychology and anthropology; but they are not yet sufficiently developed to be helpful tools in winning the war—certainly not our own war as outlined in this book.

Similarly, many excellent anthropological and other studies have been made upon primitive cultures. To hold the present study to manageable proportions, these too will have to be excluded.

I am well aware that my apparent prejudice against the use of the concepts mentioned above is controversial and places me in a small minority. My present point of view is merely that the *applications* of these concepts are not yet sufficiently developed to justify their use as tools in the work discussed here. Some day the progress of science may change this situation.

Some Specific Examples

After hearing all of these generalities, it would now be most helpful if the reader would take the time to focus on some specific examples; that is, if he would now read a few full, well-rounded discussions of the character of each of several nations, which he could select according to his own interest. Some excellent examples are given in the Supplement to the Bibliography of this book. Such discussions are too long to be included here. Some of the accounts listed cover only a few aspects of the character of the given nation. However, they are each full enough to present a human picture of a living organism. Each picture is therefore true and realistic in the best sense—in a way that a skeleton or an outline can never be.

I believe that the reader will agree that each of the references shown describes a people or a nation which has individuality—which in fact has a meaningful character significantly different from that of other nations. This is a character which can be understood, and which is worth knowing for intelligence estimates or for international relations.

It is highly significant that so many different authors,

each one writing about a nation with which he is personally familiar, should each one write as though the nation which he was describing had a character and a pattern of behavior which was its own and recognizable as different from that of other nations. This is indeed an argument for the validity of this concept.

Usefulness and Limitations of the Publications Listed

In the Supplement I give a selected list of references to studies on the national character of some of the nations and peoples of current or potential importance to the interests and national security of the United States. In the case of each nation, the list supplied is limited to a very few of the principal studies useful for our present purpose.

This is evidently a pioneer attempt. It is rather surprising that, as far as I can learn, no list of this kind, each entry selected primarily on the basis of its contribution to the character of a specific nation, exists either within or outside of the United States government. If such lists exist, they are certainly not widely known or used. Quite evidently this small beginning toward building up a bibliography of descriptions of national character useful in international relations *could* be and *should* be rapidly expanded and improved by the many governmental and private organizations now connected with the theoretical and practical applications of the national character concept.

The publications provided here were written from different backgrounds and with different purposes. With many of them, discussion of the national character or the spirit of the people is incidental to some other purpose which the author had in mind.

So the present reader will find few which cover everything he wants to know in just the manner that he likes best. The reader must do much selecting and exercise much judgment in getting the valuable parts out of each reference and in actively avoiding the chances of being misled.

In judging the references in the Supplement the following considerations, which include some ideals, may be helpful.

A description of national character should be based as far as possible upon intimate personal contact with the people concerned. The person making the contact, whom we may call the field representative, should be fluent in the language of the people upon whom he reports. The person actually writing the report need not be the person making the contact.

Part of the report may well be impressionistic and imaginative. Like journalism at its best, the report may properly arouse the emotions. Many aspects of human character and behavior are proper subjects for lively admiration, for pity, or for condemnation or contempt. Those traits of character which arouse lively emotions are *real elements in the situation* and need not be "averaged down." If a discussion of British character of the Victorian era stated that many of their politicians were statesmen of ability and patriotism, this would be a truthful contribution to the subject.[1] If this discussion also described a type of British politician who was stupid, selfish and heartless this would also be a contribution. There they are —some arousing our enthusiastic admiration, others our contempt. Each group had its influence on the national activities. However, if some objective, impartial, scientific, quantitative-minded, scholarly student of the social sciences should attempt to *strike an average* and so to sum up fairly the British Victorian politicians by saying, "Considered as a whole they were mediocre in ability, patriotism and service to their nation," he would be conveying an impression erroneous from every point of view.

This situation is important enough to deserve a little further discussion. Suppose I prepare a well-informed article which is in fact "A Firsthand Description of British Higher Education at Its Best." If I then give it this title, I make a worthwhile contribution to the subject. If I call it "A Firsthand Description of British Higher Education," I am not fair to the public, in that I am not trying to tell the whole truth in the title. However, I mislead only a few. Any one reading the article would say to himself: "This report covers only conditions at their best. How good is the higher education that the great mass of university students now receive?" Finally, if I should entitle and slant my article to indicate that it was really "A *Survey* of Current British Higher Education," then I might well mislead many readers unless they were critically minded. (Moral: In this field readers must always be critical.)

To take some specific examples.

1. The philosopher Santayana wrote an article entitled: "The Best in English Character" (53C). It is just that, and is a valuable little contribution.

2. Sir Ernest Barker edited a huge, but delightful collection of essays by many of the best English writers called *The Character of England* (53D). Each essayist strove to write an interesting and often amusing article on English Children, Science, Literature, etc. Each is reliable and *good as far as it goes*. After reading it one knows more than when he started. *But* all the contributors are British. It is completely uncritical. Some aspects of each situation are selected because they were the most amusing. There is no warning in this book: "This tells only part of the story." No such warning is needed because the scope of the book is evident to all. The book

has no intention to mislead, but its shortcomings as a serious study stand out. A reader would be foolish to fail to make use of these descriptions of the British, which are truthfully written by some of the best current British writers; but he would be a naïve reader indeed who would accept this one-sided account without looking hard elsewhere for the other sides.

As a final example consider Crankshaw's *Russia and the Russians* (listed in the Supplement). This is a highly impressionistic and journalistic account of some aspects of Russian character, written from some firsthand contact and with a sympathetic insight into some sides of the Russian character. It is unusually valuable; but in my opinion it has its own built-in warning signs. It is not only good but very good as far as it goes, *but* a reader should take a look also at what others think about the Russians.

Some Criteria for Evaluating Descriptions of National Character

For evaluating any descriptions of group or national character, and specifically those listed in the Supplement to the Bibliography of this book the reader should always ask the following questions:

1. *Coverage.* What parts of the subject is the writer of this description claiming to cover, and what parts does he really cover?

For example: Does a description of the British cover the upper classes only? In any description of the huge U.S.S.R., what geographical areas does he cover? What does he include under the word Russian? In any nation does he include both rural and urban people? *Always* what important parts of this picture are *not* adequately covered?

2. *Knowledge.* What sources did the writer have in

preparing this report? What important limitations did he have?

Some sources of knowledge of a given country might be: The author's birth and up-bringing in the country. Personal contacts with the people in their own country. Personal contacts with refugees, visitors, etc. Knowledge of the language. Knowledge of this country's history, literature, philosophy, religion, art, etc. Knowledge of related countries. Competence in such disciplines as geography, demography, political science, sociology, anthropology, social psychology, economics. In general, "area studies" of that geographic area.

3. *Motivation or Bias.* What national, religious, racial, political or other bias has the writer? For what purpose was this article written?

Possible bias is usually easy to spot. The degree to which the author yields to such bias may be more difficult to determine. The motive of the descriptions of national character in Northrop's *The Meeting of East and West* (42) is to describe each people's fundamental philosophy. For this it is excellent. Some motives may be to boost sales of a book or article by being sensational, rather than having a purpose to tell the truth.

4. *Honesty, Competence, Reliability.* What reputation for these virtues has the author, the publisher, and the organization from which it is issued?

These references are offered to assist each reader of this book to *form his own estimate* of the traits of national character pertinent to his own problem in his own given situation. To whatever he can learn from these references, the modern student can and *must* add his own new material, perhaps from better or more recent studies than those here listed, perhaps from classified sources, perhaps from his own interviews or his own visits to the people concerned. The list in the Supplement provides a *start*. It is a challenge for others to do better and is an invitation to everyone concerned with international relations to include a consideration of national character in all his work.

DIFFICULTIES IN USING NATIONAL CHARACTER AS AN INTELLIGENCE TOOL[1]

It is only fair to recognize that there are a number of scholars who do not feel that national character is a valid or useful concept. Their criticisms deserve serious consideration even though a large number of other workers, some of whom are quoted herein, favor the use of this concept.

I recognize certain inherent *difficulties* in the use of the concept of national character. These difficulties arise from the inevitable variations found in human beings, so that some human traits are unknowable and some reactions unpredictable. All of this leads to a certain degree of uncertainty in the utilization of national character. This should be clearly recognized. It can be minimized by careful study, but can never be entirely eliminated. In this respect the application of the concept of national character is similar to the application of the principles of business administration, or of military tactics, or of politics, or of any other human activities whatever. You

114

do not always win, but those who understand and apply the principles have a great advantage over those who do not.

Several of these criticisms have been mentioned earlier in this book. We shall now consider several other difficulties, starting with one which is closely related to the discussion of Groups in Section 5.

Difficulty 1. Diversity within a Nation Prevents Unity of Character

Writers on national character, including the present writer, may state their case somewhat as in the following simplified version:

The national character of Great Britain, say in the 1930's, was significantly different from the national character of Italy at the same period. The characters were found to be different when national character is understood to mean the predominant traits of character of the individuals in the two contrasting nations. The characters were also different when national character is understood to mean the character of Great Britain when acting as a nation, as compared with that of Italy when acting as a nation. This difference in character was sufficiently great and clear, so that the national character of each could have been used profitably by an intelligence officer or by the United States Department of State as one factor in estimating the capabilities and probable courses of action of Great Britain compared with Italy in peace or war. Some of the qualities, capabilities and courses of action which might have been considered at the outbreak of World War II, and in regard to which national character would play an important part are: stability of purpose, fighting qualities, progressive qualities as to using improved equipment and methods, patriotism (meaning willingness for self-sacrifice for the national good) and industry.

The fact that the character of a person or of a nation may change in the course of time has been discussed in Section 7.

The National Imprint or Trade Mark

Those believing in the importance of national character as a factor in foreign intelligence and all foreign relations would claim that the British had been subjected for years to certain recognized character-forming influences which were different from the character-forming influences to which the Italians had been subjected. A few of such influences—quite different for each nation—were: history, tradition, religion, climate, geographic location, education, economic situation, etc. These differences naturally resulted in a different character for each nation. The character of each nation was sufficiently definite and could have been sufficiently clearly grasped by an intelligence or foreign service officer so that he *could have expected* some of the kinds of differences in behavior which actually occurred in World War II.[2]

To such claims the objector replies that there is really little unity in the character-forming influences which act on the upper classes as compared with those affecting the laboring classes in the same nation. The objector claims that the British well-fed, well-educated, well-travelled upper classes are more like the Italian wealthy, educated, travelled upper classes in the important character-forming influences and in the resulting character, than they are like the British farm laborer with a subsistence wage, little education and no travel. This idea has often been developed by such books as *Sybil or The Two Nations* (54). Objectors claim that there is little effective uniformity in character, point of view or anything else between the ruling classes, the urban trades unionists and the rural farm laborers, respectively, of a given nation. So they claim that national character can have no useful meaning when applied to a whole nation.

This last point could only be *proved* by a colossal social science research project. Until so proven, it must remain in part a matter of informed opinion. To some extent, however, we can utilize the colossal social science experiment actually performed by history, say from 1800 to 1900. It is my opinion that in a variety of situations in this period a considerable unity of character, and resulting action, can be shown, sufficient to differentiate many nations from one another; for example, to differentiate each one of the following nations from all of the others, let us say in national character and in resulting action: United States, Great Britain, Italy, Spain, Russia, Turkey, China. In other words, the sum total of the character-forming influences puts a *national imprint* or *trademark* on the majority of all classes within each nation, so that there *is* a national character whether applied to the individuals within the nation or to the nation acting as such. For example, in the United States there is a spirit of progress and optimism so that new schemes and new products commonly get a ready hearing, on the farm or in the factory or office. By contrast, in some other countries there is a pervading spirit of tradition and disillusionment at all levels.

Like many other concepts pertaining to national character, the concept of a national imprint resulting from the sum total of the character-forming influences which affect a nation as a whole, can be most easily understood by the consideration of a small-scale analogy. The following recent experience at the Military Academy at West Point illustrates the basic idea. Authorities agreed that the West Point curriculum and educational plan should be radically revised and brought up to date. Authorities differed widely as to details. All agreed, however, on one essential, namely, that whatever changes were made the education of a cadet should continue to impart the same West Point imprint which had been a continuous characteristic of the Corps of Cadets for so many years.

Did imparting the West Point imprint mean that there would be an effort to make all of the Military Academy graduates exactly alike? Certainly not. There is an honorable place for the natural athlete and for the natural scholar, for the cadet who will excel as a unit commander, and for him who will make an excellent staff officer. However, with all this natural and desirable diversity, it is intended that each will receive a common imprint whereby each one will show a superior degree of honor, loyalty and courage, whatever his other traits of character may be. Although exceptions exist, this imprint would certainly be generally accepted as a part of the West Point character up to now.

This model illustrates in a somewhat accentuated form some of the real meaning and some of the inevitable limitations of the concept of group and national character.

Nations as Mechanisms

But to get back to the difficulty with which we started, let us take two hypothetical nations, Utopia and Arkadia. Suppose we grant for the sake of this argument that in character the upper classes, factory workers, and farm workers in Utopia are each more like their opposite numbers in Arkadia than they are like the differing classes in Utopia. It may still be true that there is a consistent and meaningful difference between the national character of the Utopians and that of the Arkadians.

To simplify the argument in order to bring the central point out clearly, suppose that elements of Utopian national character include progressiveness and optimism. We admit freely that these terms have different meanings and different results in the different classes of Utopia. Suppose too that elements of the Arkadian national character include backwardness and disillusionment. Now Utopia, like other modern nations, is not an amorphous mass of human beings all much alike. On the contrary, there is a marked division of labor. The nation as a whole may be regarded as a *mechanism* in which each class plays its proper part—the governing classes govern, the factory workers manufacture, the accountants keep the accounts, and the farmers produce the food. The classes differ widely in many traits of character and in their points of view. It is true, however, in Utopia that the governing classes govern liberally and in an atmosphere of optimism. Likewise the farmers believe in progress. They try new seeds and fertilizers. They expect a fair share of the nation's wealth and get it. Similarly with the other classes. Each demonstrates a progressive character in carrying out its own functions. Now to consider Arkadia. Suppose that there an atmosphere of backwardness, disillusionment and disunity prevails. No one trusts anyone else. Governments change frequently. There is little progress in manufacturing or in farming. Under these conditions, even though there was great diversity within each nation there would also be in each a *national pattern of behavior* which would distinguish one from the other, and an understanding of which would be of great practical importance to an intelligence or foreign service officer. It has been well said that even when a nation did not show within itself much unity, it might well show a *characteristic pattern of disunity*, which would affect its national character.

A comparison from another field will further illustrate this point. Suppose two four-wheeled vehicles corresponding to two nations. One is a high-class sports car, the other a heavy-duty truck. For the purposes of this analogy we eliminate any consideration of the process by which the vehicles or the nations came to have their present structures, as this is not pertinent, and would lead us too far afield. In this analogy we discuss only *what we actually find* on our examination.

In the sports car we find in one part after another the character of speed and elegance. The wheels do not resemble the clutch, nor does the clutch resemble the engine; but all have the characteristic imprint of elegance which is manifested by each part and by the mechanism as a whole. By contrast the wheels, clutch, engine, and so on of the truck, and the truck as a whole—all show the heavy-duty character. So a mechanism, whether a nation or a vehicle, can have an over-all character which is very real and from which one can predict over-all performance in comparison with some other mechanism in the same general category. This is true, even though *the parts within the given mechanism may differ* widely from each other. The same comparison could be made between the limbs and organs of a thoroughbred race horse, as compared with those of a heavy draught horse.

Difficulty 2. Variations in Accounts of National Character

It is a fact that different observers, commenting on the character of a given people from time to time, have sometimes given widely varying reports. This has been considered to throw doubt upon the reliability of the conclusions which may be drawn regarding the national character of any given country. Actually these reporters had different backgrounds, different personal, political, religious and other cultural prejudices, and different purposes for their travel and reporting. They *made no attempt to prepare reports which would be comparable with one another.* To take an extreme example, suppose an enthusiastic fisherman travelled through some of the wilder parts of Canada and reported, "This is a wonderful country." Suppose another traveller, who prized his creature comforts and did not fish, passed through the same area and reported, "This is a miserable country. I should recommend it only to my worst enemies." Such discrepancies would not cast doubt upon the ability of travellers to make reliable reports *if they started with the same ground rules.*

Incidentally a set of ground rules for investigating and reporting on the national character of certain types of peoples, so as to obtain comparable results and increase the number of intelligence bull's eyes scored in the judgments of national character, would be a worthy object for anyone responsible for area studies, and especially for an intelligence or foreign service officer.

This would make an ambitious, but rewarding, subject for the term project of a student at the Army War College or the National War College. It would be desirable as a research project in the social sciences at a civilian university, or as a government-sponsored research to be carried out at RAND or elsewhere.[3]

Even without any uniform ground rules to make possible comparable reports on national character, a surprising (but certainly not perfect) degree of agreement in the reports pertaining to a given country often occurs. A very recent example is *As Others See Us: The United States through Foreign Eyes,* edited by Franz M. Joseph (55). In this book twenty observers from Europe, Asia, Africa and the Americas report independently on the

United States. Most of these observers are highly competent, and some like Denis Brogan are well-known. In spite of their diversity of outlook there is considerable agreement in the picture presented. Professor Arthur M. Schlesinger, Jr., in his review of this book (56) shows that the present picture is much like the "composite portrait of the United States" which his father presented seventeen years earlier as emerging out of the accounts of foreign travelers here since 1782.

All of this emphasizes the strength and continuity of the characteristic central core of the pattern of national behavior in America, even when the picture is drawn from reporters widely separated in time and national background.

One of the fundamental difficulties in utilizing the concept of national character is certainly the difficulty which every writer experiences in making clear to the reader his own understanding of the character of a people. The writer may have lived among these people for twenty years. He may speak their language and have a real gift for the sympathetic understanding of foreign peoples. Yet no well-tried, ready-made form exists by which he can make clear to the reader his own intimate understanding of what kind of people these really are. Correspondingly, readers of reports on national character may have to give an unusual amount of critical thought to such reports in order to discover what the writer really means.

Difficulty 3. Patterns in Human Behavior Have Been Overdone

Finally, we reach an important, but rather diffuse and nebulous objection to using judgments of national character in intelligence estimates on foreign policy. Some people, like Toynbee (57), think that they see definite patterns in human history. Other people feel that patterns, regularity and meaning in history have been greatly overdone. Some of these critics of Toynbee claim that the patterns "seen" in history are due to selection and to twisting the data to fit the theory. Some of these critics go so far as to state that each event in history is unique and tells us little or nothing about what to expect elsewhere. Such people would object to the claim that any meaningful, reliable, statements can be made about national character. They almost imply that there is nothing to be learned from experience.

I take here a middle ground with a completely pragmatic point of view. As already stated, I believe that the utilization of national character in all foreign relations is closely similar to using our judgment of individual character in our personal relations. We know that our judgment is not infallible. We know just as clearly that it is usually helpful. So we make as much use of such judgment as we can in our personal relations. Similarly, in using national character, we shall try to get out of it all the value that there is in it. By so doing we may win a real advantage over the country that neglects this source of help.

One difference between judging national character and judging personal character lies in the fact that national character is more difficult to estimate. There is evidently much still to be learned about methods for judging national character from systematic studies in this field. Experience again demonstrates, however, that elements of many situations show a usable consistency, and that patterns of national behavior are profitable fields of study.

LEVELS OF INVESTIGATION
LEADING TO TOP
ACHIEVEMENT

What must we do to form an estimate of the character of a given nation? What confidence can we place in our conclusions? How much usable intelligence benefit and international understanding can we hope to acquire? And as the subject of this section, what are the *requirements for top achievement* in this field?

For practical, operational purposes, we find that an investigation of national character can be undertaken at three successive levels. Each level is more trouble than the one before it. Each requires *greater ability* and deals with problems where intelligence judgment plays a more important part than in the preceding level. Top achievement in the interpretation of national character is the great goal which we now set before ourselves.

First and simplest, as a different approach, we might consider the three *psychological* levels pertaining to character studies, as they are discussed in Sections 3, 5 and 6. We can attempt to judge the character of persons, groups or nations:

(a) Principally by their characteristic patterns of *behavior*.

(b) We can go deeper and look also for underlying *motives*.

(c) Finally we can dig down as far as science and insight will take us, to include an understanding of the Fundamental Philosophy of the people concerned, and the *insight based upon personal contact*.

A consideration of these psychological levels gives us perspective and understanding in this field; but this psychological classification cuts across the developments actually encountered in the conduct of any specific research project which involves national character. Real-life projects do not follow this "tidy" pattern.

It is by no means necessary to organize an elaborate research project into the national character of a given nation, or to be a professional anthropoligist, in order to get benefits of great value from an investigation of the character of the people concerned in any question of foreign intelligence or foreign relations. In fact, much is gained if the worker in either of these fields will simply ask himself the question: What effect—beneficial or otherwise—will the character of the people concerned have upon the activities under consideration?

In any study of this kind the data from various sources must be put together with the benefit of wide knowledge, professional competence and judgment, to result in real understanding.

We now turn to a consideration of the three levels of investigation from a different point of view, namely, the three levels of systematic, organized intelligence projects, or studies in international relations. If we as individuals or the United States government, due to faulty methods, must do a superficial job, we should be aware of its shortcomings.

Analogy with Investigations of Personal Character

As so often happens when discussing national or group character, it is helpful to start with analogies in personal character. So it is now useful to consider investigations of personal character at three levels for comparison.

First is the informal sizing up of the character of another person. This is the kind that many corporations carry out when they are recruiting recent college graduates for junior positions. The candidate presents a simple statement of verifiable facts, including his age, nationality, education, extracurricular activities, jobs held (if any), special skills, and hobbies. An interview gives some further ideas of his intelligence, ability to express himself clearly, and perhaps of his adaptability and likeability. An investigation of character at this level is short and inexpensive. It deals with facts which are open to all. It requires no technical knowledge. To a reasonably experienced recruiter it tells a great deal. But there are evidently many areas completely untouched.

As a second level let us consider the investigation that one might make of a stranger considered as a business partner, or for a high executive position in a corporation, or as a customer for a large personal loan. Here one would get a careful report from a credit organization such as Dun and Bradstreet. Such reports contain much besides financial ratings. There are statements regarding the candidate's standing in the community, his associates, family difficulties, perhaps about any rumored questionable activities. Such an investigation takes more time. It requires an organization experienced in such work. Briefly, it costs more and tells us more. Such an elaborate investigation is worthwhile for the purposes named, but is certainly unnecessary for a corporation when hiring a young engineer as a junior draftsman, for example.

At the third and highest level take the "clearance" investigations undertaken to clear a man for a position requiring the handling of papers classified up to Top Secret. Here we are justified in digging into nearly all important aspects of a man's experience and character, including psychological considerations. We look for possible hidden or discreditable factors. This takes much time, skill and money, but under the circumstances we could not feel satisfied with anything less.

General Considerations for all Levels of Investigation

For *all* levels of investigations into national character we assume as a minimum that we start with an experienced intelligence officer or foreign service officer with some knowledge of modern history, of the social sciences, and of intelligence production principles and methods, or of foreign service requirements.

At any one of the levels of investigation at which an intelligence officer is working, he will say to himself from time to time as his work proceeds:

"As far as I can see, the pertinent traits of character of this nation are the following. . . .

"Now let me see what I can find against my present tentative conclusions as above mentioned."

And later: "My final conclusions regarding character being so and so, how will these traits of character tend to influence the capabilities, probable courses of action, and other conclusions in this paper?"

Even if he went no further, something would already have been gained by the very fact that this investigator had given some serious and *systematic* consideration to this great intangible known as national character as one factor when estimating what a given nation would really accomplish when that nation used the hard facts of its natural resources, weapons and institutions, or what decisions it would make under given conditions.

However, it should be evident by this time that for best results, judgments of national character as a factor in foreign intelligence estimates or in international relations should be made by someone who has made a special study of this subject and who is already familiar with the characters of other nations, preferably those somewhat similar to the nation now under study. From this earlier experience the worker in this field can expect three specific advantages:

First, a prior familiarity with the principles and methods of any subject saves time in working with it. He should bring to his new project some knowledge of the principles and methods of anthropology and political science, and of the variations in different aspects of national character which different investigators have recorded, and the indications of these traits of character which are usually observable. He then knows at the start what kinds of indications to look for and where to look. But he should not be content to look only for the conventional and expected traits of character.

Second, in foreign intelligence production and foreign relations, one can seldom make field tests or hold extensive interviews with "natives." Data are usually scanty, crucial facts may be unobtainable. This is another case where "success comes not so much in holding a good hand, but from playing a poor hand well." In other words a man experienced in working with national character will best be able to see the significance of data at hand and to make the most profitable use of what he has available. He can fit scattered facts into the kind of picture that he knows usually exists because he has built up similar pictures in similar cases. Prior experience or training can guide him in this activity as it does in other activities.

Third, perspective and a worthwhile judgment of the reliability and significance of evidence of national character in a given case come only when the investigator can compare data found for the nation under study, with data previously recorded for other nations. These other nations preferably include some from the same general area. For example a comparison among themselves of the observed characters of different Latin American countries, or of Middle Eastern countries. It is also helpful, where possible, to compare the observations on the character of the country under study, perhaps behind the Iron Curtain, with some known country having points of similarity. We gain the great advantage of going from the known to the unknown.

So in this field as in so many others the ability to make comparisons multiplies the value of the conclusions and is some check on their probable reliability. In judging national character, "He knows not England, who only England knows."

All of these general considerations pertain to each of the levels of investigation which are discussed in the remainder of this section. All of these considerations are assumed to be operative in each of the levels of investigation described.

The First Level in Estimating National Character

For the first level we assume an intelligent and somewhat experienced analyst or intelligence officer as described above. He is not familiar with the language of the nation concerned nor has he been there. He has made no special prior study of national character, nor has he specialized on area studies in this general area. He naturally reads what travellers to that country have said, but he does not have available for active assistance on this specific paper anyone who knows the country firsthand.

Evidently much will depend upon the time available for his study. An equal amount will depend upon his experience and judgment in using his time to best advantage. Much will depend upon the knowledge which he happens to bring to the study; and much upon his imagination in putting the available facts together to form a coherent picture of conditions and activities and probable developments. He will not have time to delve into basic beliefs, or the character of different groups, nor into the mechanism of the action of these groups within the nation under study.

From available books, articles and other documents in a limited time he can put together a careful and conscientious, but plodding, limited and uninspired statement. He can say, "Based upon recent actions, the character and probable developments will be so and so." He will be greatly handicapped in not having a chance to exchange ideas by letter or in person with one who has been there. He will always wonder how his long-range guesses will look to someone who knows the country by personal contact.

Not having any special foundation from education or experience in the study of national character, he will not know what to look for in studying this aspect of his problem, nor will he make most skilful use of the data on this subject which would be helpful to a more experienced man. Not having much basis for comparing the character of the given nation with others, his judgment on national character will have limited value.

A very serious handicap to his knowledge will be the

present well-known caution of United States Foreign Service officers on the spot to state their real opinions, even in confidential communications, for fear of getting themselves into trouble (58).

As a result of the general situation described, an intelligence officer or other analyst working on this first level might well remain ignorant of recent developments below the surface. Such developments might indicate the approach of vital changes in the previously existing situation, yet this previous situation could easily continue to be accepted in the general atmosphere of official opinion. These weaknesses in the reports at the first (lowest) level should be recognized. It is like hiring a man as a personal assistant whom you have never seen. You have his record with all the *facts* regarding age, degrees, and so forth, but you must still wonder *what sort of man he really is.*

To sum up: On the first level a good analyst or any other student of foreign affairs with considerable time, but with no special knowledge of the particular country, can get a fair picture of the national character based upon its characteristic patterns of behavior in the past. He knows little about the motivation and mechanism which brought about such behavior. He has no special training in national character, and little comparative judgment. His understanding will seldom enable him to estimate how the behavior would probably change under changing conditions. He is probably somewhat blind to recent changes below the surface. This level is an example of the kind of amateurish approach we sometimes find in governmental investigations of such problems.

The Second Level

At this level we assume a good intelligence officer or member of the United States Department of State, or advanced student of foreign affairs who has specialized in the nation under study, or at least in this general area. Through active team co-operation, he can bring to bear upon his study knowledge of the language. He already has a considerable mature knowledge of the country's geography, history, politics, economics, military situation, institutions and principal men. He has a little knowledge of its literature and traditions.

He may have had little or no chance to live in the country of his specialization. He can perhaps get some co-operation from foreign service officers or others who have been there. He may be definitely weak on a vital factor in understanding character: namely, personal contact with the people and institutions.

In general at this level an ordinarily good man in the employ of the United States government can in theory bring to bear upon his study of the national character of a given nation all of the resources of the U.S. government which he can ordinarily expect to have available to him. These resources are large. We start with the library services, map services, microfilm services, reproduction services, etc., which are in general excellent and available. Then there are huge masses of pertinent information and intelligence, open and classified, about each foreign country scattered through the files of the Department of State, Department of Defense, the Central Intelligence Agency and many other government departments and agencies. Can he find what he needs and can he get his hands on it with the expenditure of a reasonable amount of time and effort, even if he has the necessary security clearance? His results from such an effort would vary all the way from excellent to zero, depending first upon the support which he could get from his own superiors, and second upon his personal skill at forcing his way through red tape. Finally and perhaps more important than any written words, there would certainly exist among all the hordes of government employees living in the Washington area some persons who had lived in or visited the country concerned. For these one would think first of those connected with the Department of State, next the armed services, next the huge number of other government services which send members abroad in connection with foreign aid, United States Information Agency, agriculture, etc. The chances of finding and getting a chance to talk with someone who knew the country firsthand might well be invaluable to any one concerned with national character. Yet little has been done to make available to those in the government who need it this great asset toward the understanding of foreign countries. An up-to-date card catalog and streamlined facilities for making such contacts with those who had been to the country concerned would add immeasurably to the soundness of our basic understanding of foreign peoples.

From history he knows as a matter of solid fact the country's characteristic patterns of behavior under various conditions. From a more detailed knowledge of groups, institutions, and key men within the country he can usually form a reliable picture of the pressure groups and political mechanisms which can bring about or prevent action in the country. His opinion as to underlying motives is worth considering, but could be made better.

By taking an interest in traits of national character and then asking himself specific questions, and then taking the trouble to look for well-grounded answers, he can build up a reliable picture of many aspects of national character based on data from the very recent past. What evidence is there of a progressive spirit, of unity or disunity on important matters, of a will-to-win in the face of difficulties, of a good-neighbor policy, of integrity in high places, and so forth? Most questions like these have answers which can be known with considerable confidence.

Through reports of travellers, diplomatic dispatches, literature and traditions, our intelligence area specialist can form some idea of their basic beliefs and their manner of thought—all so important in judging character.

In summary, even in the imperfect world in which we must carry out our mission, this intelligence officer or foreign service officer or advanced student can benefit to a greater or less extent from *every procedure* mentioned in the present study for understanding national character. The character of individuals, groups and of the nation acting as such are available for study. The mechanism by which groups act within the nation can be discovered. Underlying motives can be estimated with less certainty. He forms some idea of basic beliefs and knows something of the modes of thought in this country. He is still weak in that kind of understanding which comes only from personal contact with the nation in question: namely, in his insight into hidden prospective changes of character, and in answering the nebulous but tremendously important question: After all, what kind of people are they?

Adding it all up, an intelligence officer or area studies scholar operating at this second level can make solid and highly important contributions to our estimates of foreign countries.

The Third (Highest) Level

A Utopia wherein only great men operate in a perfect world has no interest or value whatever as a background for studying foreign intelligence or foreign relations problems. However, it is definitely worthwhile to picture what we could properly hope to achieve if some parts of the intelligence community or the foreign service operated *as well as is now actually done* in some other large fields of human endeavor—such varied fields, for example, as some progressive corporations, the better scientific and engineering societies, research departments in the natural sciences at the leading universities, and in the United States Regular Army. So the following picture of possible progress might be useful in pointing out certain goals worth striving for.

In the procedures for studying national character at this highest level we shall consider improvement in just three aspects of this operation. These are:

1. As in other disciplines, workers from whom top-level results are expected should have the benefit of the best possible education *in their own profession.* Amateurs usually get only amateurish results.
2. Specialists should be selected for outstanding ability and should each one be given the opportunity to concentrate his efforts upon some important country or geographic area.
3. The quality of the contacts of United States government representatives with each foreign country should be greatly improved, preferably through the Foreign Service,[1] so that the United States government will gain more intimate pictures of the life and thought of foreign peoples than is now usually the case.

The first proposed improvement (better training in intelligence production) has been discussed elsewhere

(38, pp. 256-264). It is self-evident. Similar improvements in the formal educational courses of the Foreign Service Institute are needed. Professional standards should be higher.

If the second improvement (expert area knowledge) were made, we could approach the great goal for judging national character by which a specialist in Poland, let us say, can be so steeped in Polish literature and traditions that he can, to some degree, "think like a Pole." Finally and most important of all is the third proposed improvement for closer contacts between our foreign service officers and the countries to which they are accredited. For example, only intimate contact with the Poles will make evident to those on the spot the beginnings of *important changes below the surface* in national character. For such insight we should be able to rely upon members of our foreign service who lived with the Poles for years. If this fails, then arrangements must be made for other selected specialists to live in the country of their specialty for a year or more in some capacity.

With these changes we would have for each foreign country the most competent specialist that could be found or developed. We would be in a better position than at present to detect evidence of impending change in character. Evidently this requires effective co-operation among several different kinds of specialists. The problems of intellectual teamwork have been studied by several civilian research organizations.

To approach our ideal for comprehending national character anew and slightly differently, let us start with C. P. Snow's (60) comment that the judgment of the character of an individual based upon the intellect alone is "the shallowest kind." Similarly judgment of the character of a nation based only upon hard facts and overt behavior comes from the intellect alone and is apt to be shallow and inadequate. Much deeper insight arises from the fuller study of national character which is described under the second and third levels. The profoundest insight, and therefore the most reliable estimates, comes from a knowledge of hard facts combined with a knowledge of the character, based not only on the intellect, but *also* upon a sympathetic understanding of that nation and some ability to think like it, derived from a familiarity with its literature and traditions and from personal contacts. This helps to give a deeper and a more well-rounded picture. We would then be in a position to get the full benefit of our understanding of the national character including basic beliefs for any intelligence or foreign relations purpose.

As a general summary of this section: National character may be studied at three different levels, depending upon the time allowed, the competence of the personnel available and upon the importance of the problem. At the elementary level any educated man can make contributions of some value. At the highest level, where we require deep insight into present conditions and also indications of coming changes, high standards of professional competence, comparable to those found in the best universities is required. Effective teamwork of specialists in at least three different fields is necessary. This is always difficult to obtain. In its requirements for top level achievement, foreign intelligence or foreign service is just like other intellectual pursuits. It requires the best efforts of the best men to get the best results.

From an entirely different approach, one of the basic needs for better use of national character in foreign intelligence and foreign relations is more *appreciation of its value* as one essential factor in a given situation. This appreciation must exist at the working level. It is even more important at the higher levels, namely, on the part of those responsible for training, for the production of papers, and for active operations. With a little more support in these higher quarters, improvements in the present situation would speedily appear.

CRITICAL REVIEW OF
TENTATIVE CONCLUSIONS

In all fields of study where conclusions must be drawn regarding human actions, a final critical review by several persons with diverse backgrounds should be a normal part of the process.

Two-sided Discussions

Conant (61) makes a suggestion in a slightly different connection which would be applicable here. He says:

> First of all, a healthy skepticism is in order in listening to an expert, particularly an enthusiastic one. The next step is to try to find a person of equal technical competence but with an opposite emotional bias. If such a one is not at hand, some competent individual hitherto unconcerned with whatever project is in question should be asked to undertake the job of being "devil's advocate," as it were. He should be asked to devote himself to preparing the case for the reasoned opposition to what has been proposed. . . .
> This is not the time nor place for me to outline in detail my remedy for what many feel to be a bad situation. I will content myself by saying I believe that if the Department of

139

Defense would gradually introduce a quasijudicial system of review which provided forced opposition to new projects, the taxpayers' money would be more wisely spent. When a question came up to be settled, even if three or four echelons from the top, one or two referees or judges might hear the arguments pro and con. The important point is that there should be arguments against the proposal; they should be vigorous but candid; . . . Then adequate briefs for the two sides could be prepared (not compromise committee reports). With opposing briefs, arguments, and cross-questioning, many facets of the problem, many prejudices of the witnesses would be brought out into the open. The forced opposition is the important point.

If we should apply Conant's basic suggestion, then when an important intelligence estimate or report pertaining to foreign relations is submitted for approval some person should be assigned to play the "devil's advocate," as it were, and to present a well-prepared criticism of the paper under discussion, pointing out weaknesses, questioning the data, and challenging the assumptions and conclusions where appropriate.

The ensuing discussion between the author of the paper and the officially appointed critic—held in the presence of the reviewing authority and any others who could helpfully be present—would have some resemblance to a legal case argued before a Court of Appeals. The weak points would probably be exposed. Strong points would stand out from their very ability to resist attack. Important sides to the question, not properly considered by the author, might be returned to him for further study and report. Some alternative conclusions might be found preferable to the conclusions proposed in the first draft. In papers touching on national character the critic would ask, whenever appropriate, what search had been made for evidence of an approaching change in character.

As I have said elsewhere: "This is in accordance with the military experience with a two-sided map problem or two-sided maneuver as far superior to a one-sided exercise controlled by umpires. The two-sided exercise is also much more trouble in both military or intelligence problems, but the extra trouble is more than justified by the higher quality of the results" (38).

Many criticisms like those indicated above are now voiced in the numerous reviews through which an intelligence estimate goes before final approval. However, these reviews are to some extent haphazard. No one has the *specific responsibility* to smoke out the weak spots of a specific kind. Points that happen to catch the attention of the reviewers attract the most fire. Superficial weaknesses seldom escape. Under the present system of review no one except the author has the specific duty to dig below the surface for the more deep-seated fallacies. We lack the healthy smoking-out of weak points which comes from the two-sided war-gaming of a military problem.

One of the great needs for progress in understanding in such fields as foreign intelligence is *the need for intellectual team work,* whereby several minds, each with a different approach, are brought to bear on one problem. Conant's proposed method would be worth trying as a step in this direction.

I have discussed elsewhere some applications of this to intelligence production. I say: "Further use of the two-sided problem in cases of importance is probably one of the most promising opportunities for making substantial improvement in the results of Strategic Intelligence Production" (38, pp. 124-127).

A critical review of the kind just described is *doubly* necessary in conclusions pertaining to national character. This for two reasons:

First: for any given nation, the data pertaining to its

national character are as widespread as the nation. The aspects are many and various including the political economic, military, and cultural activities of that nation. In such a situation the opinions of several well-informed persons are likely to be much better than one. In such a panel of critics, the discussion of a dissenting opinion will often bring out how well-founded, or the reverse, are the tentatively approved conclusions.

Second: and most important, is the need to search for evidence of a possible approaching change. This will now be considered.

The Search for Approaching Change

In another activity, namely the stock market, the big question often is: When will the present bull market become a bear market? In the stock market, and in the judgments of national character, many observers fall into the natural error of believing that a trend which has continued for a long time, will continue for a long time more. In the stock market, in intelligence, and in matters of foreign policy, some of the greatest disasters have arisen from falling into this error. (For example, the error of assuming that the fighting spirit of the French in World War I would be repeated in World War II.) Great prizes in the stock market, in intelligence production, and in foreign relations go to the man or the nation respectively who can detect indications of change while these evidences are still below the surface. One important indication of possible approaching change in national character is a modification in the make-up of the governing classes. Under present world conditions radical changes of many kinds now take place with a frequency and rapidity unknown in any other period of history. Unusual developments are no longer unusual.

Some Causes and Indications of Approaching Change

A marked change in the character of persons, groups, or nations must always eventually bring about changes in their activities. Otherwise, personal, group, and national character would be only abstract concepts without operational meaning. However, the converse is not necessarily true. A change in activities does not always imply a change in character. For example, in a nation ruled by a dictator, assassination may lead to the replacement of a war-like dictator by one who is peaceful, crafty, and avaricious, without any immediate change in the character of the people as a whole.

It *is* true, however, that marked changes in the structure, policies, activities, thoughts and loyalties of a group or a nation are often indications of a change in character. If so, such changes are probably forerunners of much more extensive changes to follow. These may include political, industrial, social, military and other fields. Real changes in character generally have rather far-reaching, long-range operational effects.

All forms of government and all ruling classes are subject to change, slow or rapid. In the study of international affairs the possibility of unexpected shifts must always be considered. (Perhaps they should sometimes even be expected.)

When changes occur in national policy and action of the kind discussed here, there is actually interaction and some confusion between personal character, national character, national policy, and national action. As one simple example, consider the personal character of citizens and the national character of the United States as to warlike qualities in the early days of World War I as it was then being waged in Europe, say 1914, 1915 and

1916. Very briefly, the personal character of citizens as a nation and national character of the United States were outstandingly peace-loving. However, as the war continued many events connected with the war outraged the American people and built up a considerable war spirit. This brought about a change in our character as a nation. One evidence of this was the declaration of war by the United States in 1917. This national action, accompanied by the war atmosphere and propaganda, certainly led to a more warlike American personal character. These changes ran more or less parallel to changes in national policy. All of this is an example of *interdetermination* discussed in Appendix B.

The foregoing picture of a change in individual character with accompanying changes in national character and national policy has been highly simplified. It is nevertheless confusing. It is not "tidy" as the British say. In regard to any given statements, it is often difficult to say: This one refers to national character; that one to national policy. Such an analysis could be made, but it would be difficult, and full of qualifying phrases. Perhaps the word-picture drawn here is no more confusing than the actual operations which it attempts to describe.

So we may regard the description of changes in national character, and in organization, in policy, and in action as changes which are often observed to be *associated together* in a cause and/or effect relationship. (Please turn again to Appendix B.)

All of this has the following highly practical applications. An intelligence officer or foreign service officer should be constantly on the lookout for evidences of coming changes. In a foreign country, much of what is happening is below the surface. He cannot conduct psychological tests of the inhabitants, nor carry out a "content analysis" of their secret files. He must make the most of whatever evidence he can collect. Much of what follows here, dealing as it does with the leadership, is more apt to become generally known. From changes at the top, the officer is taught to expect certain other hidden changes below the surface. In fact, when this officer encounters any of these indications of possible change, he would be led to look around for the other changes which usually accompany it.

In theory we might be able to consider separately changes in personal character, in national character, and in national action, by imagining a simplified situation in which the high lights would be somewhat as follows: In a people like the Arab peoples which have been backward for centuries, new developments lead to a change in the personal character of a large number of the leaders. From being hopeless, passive and pessimistic, they become hopeful, aggressive and optimistic. Such a change in personal character is relatively stable. This tendency to stability will usually continue and will continue to exert pressure through many political ups and downs. For example, under present world conditions, we can imagine many temporary changes in the national policy of some Arab nations;[1] but we can hardly imagine that they will return to the character which they possessed a hundred years ago. A deep-seated change in personal character tends to lead, after some delay and after many temporary changes in direction, to a corresponding change in the *character of the nations* acting as such. This change in national character may lead again after many ups and downs eventually to a change in national policy. National policy, however, is governed by many caprices and powerful factors, of which national character is only one. Many times the national policy and national actions have for a while shown no rational connection with national character or even with the evident needs of the nation.

Thus, in any *given* situation the foreign intelligence or foreign relations officer will often be able to trace these different threads of action as far as is necessary to clarify his particular problem.

If this officer encounters some of the indications here mentioned, then the later parts of this section, and Sections 5, 7 and Appendix B will tell him what other related changes will be worth looking for. This will focus his attention on some likely clues. We cannot tell him what he will find.

Studies in history, political science, or government describe such changes, and so enable an intelligence or foreign service officer to recognize the first indications of a possible shift. An excellent study of this kind is Lasswell and Kaplan's (27) chapter on "Process." This describes the causes, initial stages, progress, and final results of many kinds of military, political and social revolutions or lesser changes.[2] Some of the definitions, concepts and conclusions from this chapter will indicate what may often be discovered when an important deviation from past performance is approaching. Some of this is presented below in direct quotations because these authors are describing specifically the processes which we have in mind, and their wording can hardly be improved.

[*Crisis*] Crisis is precipitated, not merely by conflict, but by the failure of available practices for the resolution of conflict. . . . Breakdown is not the result of special interests dividing the community, but rather of the particular maladjustments which prevent compromise between these interests.

[*Contraction of Elite*] As the situation approaches crisis
. . . the elite contracts, power becoming concentrated in the
hands of the initially most powerful segment of the elite.
The lesser holders relinquish their share in the expectation
of a more expedient and indulgent resolution of the crisis....

[*Elite Recruitment*] Elite recruitment in a crisis situation
tends to be based on skills appropriate to a resolution of the
crisis favorable to the elite. Sections of the elite recruited
on the basis of other skills . . . suffer corresponding depriva-
tion of power position. . . .

Whether or not a rule is stable depends on the ability of
the elite to recruit itself with a minimum of dissent. Such
circulation of the elite can continue only so long as the ideology in the name of which it exercises its authority, per-
sists, and the peaceful replacements in the elite are difficult
in proportion as adherence to the ideology weakens in intensity. Thus . . . the maintenance of power depends on
adherence to the political doctrine under which it is exer-
cised.

[*A Measure of the Quality of Intelligence*] In the internal
affairs of a State, party leaders concentrate on the elements
within the party or outside that are assumed to be most
promising for or most threatening against their power.

Discrepancies between the focus of attention and the
facts measure the degree to which the intelligence function
has failed to give decision makers what they require as a
basis of realistic judgment. Probably no inquiries into the
processes of politics are more rewarding than the study of
factors that contribute to such discrepancies. We know that
professional diplomats and soldiers make disastrous errors
because of unrealistic perspectives. Imperial states have
sometimes met unanticipated resistance, and party leaders
notoriously are led into frequent error by depending upon
optimistic reports from party hacks.

We must not, of course, attach exclusive importance to
the breakdown of the intelligence function as a source of
erroneous decisions. Often the foreign diplomatic and mili-

tary missions have brought accurate reports which have been ignored because the elites were too sluggish, inefficient, or ignorant to use them.

[*Change in the Ruling Class*] Ruling classes decline inevitably when they cease to find scope for the capacities through which they rose to power, when they can no longer render the social services which they once rendered, or when their talents and the services they render lose in importance in the social environment in which they live. . . .

A class considered as a whole never spontaneously surrenders its position of advantage. It never recognizes any moral reason sufficiently powerful to compel it to abdicate in favor of its "poorer brethren." [3]

Many of the most important indications of change are in the realm of thoughts, belief and feelings—emphasizing again the need to have foreign representatives who know the peoples of each foreign country sufficiently intimately to have an insight into their feelings.

[*Lack of Faith*] Stability requires intense adherence to the political doctrine not only on the part of the mass, but of the elite as well. . . . Michels put the matter with characteristic emphasis. . . . "We may regard it as an established historical law that races, legal systems, institutions, and social classes, are inevitably doomed to destruction from the moment they or those who represent them have lost faith in their future."

For among other reasons, this lack of faith on the part of the elite will be communicated to the mass, whose support for the power structure will thereupon diminish proportionately. Moreover the political doctrine serves as a basis of solidarity for the elite. . . . And in turn, this lack of solidarity weakens resistance against the potential threat of rival elites.

Indications

The above discussion points out some of the specific places where it is necessary to look for hidden indications of possible change in a foreign government, besides the more evident dramatic events which make the headlines. Such changes in nations often accompany changes in national character as Cause and/or Effect (See Appendix B).

As a summary we note that indications of a possible change are seen:

When means for compromise between conflicting interests are lacking.

When an elite contracts and concentrates power in a few.

When recruitment of an elite is not based on skills appropriate to the resolution of a crisis.

When the elite has difficulty in recruiting peaceably its own kind to fill vacancies.

When party leaders fail to focus the attention of the workers on those factors critical for success.

When the ruling class fails to find acceptance for the kind of service which its members once rendered.

When important changes occur in the kind of persons recruited for the ruling classes and the elite.

When the ruling classes, the elite or the masses lose faith in the accepted doctrine and in the future.

These examples will suggest the existence of many other indications of equal value in this search.

The Lone Wolf

In the Intelligence Community and in the Foreign Service the officer who reports signs of a coming change must not only be right, he must also be convincing, courageous and persistent. The burden of proof is upon him. A report of a coming change conflicts with the prevailing opinion, upsets current plans, and so is often highly unwelcome. The common tendency to resist new ideas makes some officers hesitate to report information or to sponsor conclusions which will be contrary to the status quo.

Yet it is essential to have some officers with the originality, insight, and courage required to challenge axioms, and worse still, to challenge current or entrenched official opinion.

When some new development in national character or in national achievements finally breaks out so as to become common knowledge, a healthy and instructive exercise consists in a search of the records to find out who were among the first to point out the change in the wind, which has now occurred and is evident to all, and what reception their forecasts then received, and why.

An informal search of this kind in some of the British foreign intelligence files shows forecasts of the coming growth of Arab nationalism as early as the 1920's. Acceptance of the new picture was slow and encountered the expected opposition. Earlier indications were available. Even as early as February, 1914, at the time of Amir Abdullah's visit to Lord Kitchener and Sir Ronald Storrs in Cairo, Storrs was able to detect indications of a coming change as noted in his memoirs (63). With our present hindsight we realize that more of the diplomats assigned to the Middle East might well have foreseen the present developments in the Arab world earlier and much more clearly than was actually realized.

We should not wait until we stumble over indications of such a change by chance. On the contrary, we should go on an active search for such indications. We should look for exceptions to the usual actions. We should not ignore awkward objects that look out of place in the pretty picture which gives the conventional view of a given nation. There is even a whole book on *The Art of Contrary Thinking* (62).

So in the course of the preparation of any foreign relations study involving national character, the investigator might well say to himself: "These are my tentative conclusions. They are in line with the prevailing opinion and are about what we have always expected. Now let me see what evidence I can find in opposition, and especially what evidence there is of an impending change."

Under present fluid world conditions, in every intelligence or foreign service team, the rebel, the dissenter, the unfortunate lone wolf should play an important part, and *must be given support.* A.J.P. Taylor (64), speaking of the British, says that today's ideas about foreign policy have usually been borrowed from the unpopular pronouncements of yesterday's Dissenters.[4] Even if this statement is exaggerated, it is well worth stopping to think about.

EXAMPLES OF THE
UNIQUE ROLE OF
NATIONAL CHARACTER
IN INTELLIGENCE

I give now several examples to illustrate and to support my claim that a consideration of national character often contributes new and vital factors in an international situation which cannot be obtained from any other source. In some cases these new factors are *in direct opposition* to evidence from such other sources, so that the new factors necessitate a radical change in the over-all conclusions.

The following examples are selected primarily because they throw light upon *this peculiar quality* of national character as an intelligence or foreign service tool. It is *different in kind* from most of the conventional components of strategic intelligence, which latter can often be largely expressed in terms of objective facts and figures.

After all that has been said in this book, it should be unnecessary to state again that national character is never the only factor in a problem of foreign intelligence or foreign relations. In these complicated fields, national character can never be more than one of several factors to be considered. Equally unnecessary to state should be the fact that in these fields, as in every other field dealing with human relations, there is always a chance for error or difference of opinion. In these fields we deal with evidence rather than with proof. Such being the case, it is true here, as in other similar fields, that when evidence is corroborated by more and more other evidence, the probability that it contains valuable elements of truth increases.

Example 1. The Soviet Decision to Sign a Pact with Germany, 1939

In 1939 when Hitler's Germany was a growing threat to the nations of Europe and the shadow of the Second World War was growing darker, the British sent a mission to Moscow to arrange for some measures of co-operation between Britain and the U.S.S.R. The British mission in Moscow was apparently making good progress when they were astounded to hear in August that the Soviets had just signed an agreement with Ribbentrop to co-operate with Germany instead of with Britain.

Later in the war—in August, 1942—Churchill had the opportunity for an informal and rather intimate conversation with Stalin. This meeting is described by Bryant (65) and Churchill (66). Churchill asked Stalin why the Russians had let the British down and sided with the Germans in 1939. Stalin replied in effect as follows:

> We Russians knew in detail the military weakness of you British at that time. We knew how bad the French Army was, and how little reliance could be placed in it and we thought you must know it also. Under these circumstances, we Russians thought that the British and the French must

be bluffing in their promise to support Poland. We could not imagine that you British would fulfill your agreements and would really declare war in the face of such well-known military weaknesses. So we Russians temporarily sided with the Germans.

Even granted that this answer lacked candor, and was only part of the truth in the light of the disorganized condition of the Soviet army in 1939, nevertheless it is highly probable that the considerations named had a strong influence, as Stalin said, on the Soviet decision at that time.[1] Certainly this was Churchill's opinion.

This case is suggestive of the necessity for considering national character as a vital factor in an international situation before drawing final conclusions as a basis for action. It is significant that all of the hard facts upon which Stalin relied for his decision were correct. His knowledge of the numbers of trained troops in the British Army and the numbers of planes in the British and French Armies was correct. If he had had twice as many intelligence officers, compiling twice as many facts of this kind, he would have been just as wrong. Only by a consideration of British character could he have foreseen that the British would be stubborn enough to declare war in order to make good their commitments, and to keep on fighting when they had so little to fight with.[2]

Example 2. "The German Mind," an Essay by Ludwig, 1938

Emil Ludwig was a distinguished German-born historian who left Germany in 1907 to become a citizen of Switzerland. When the clouds which foreshadowed World War II were gathering, he wrote an article in the *Atlantic Monthly* (67) which appeared a year and a half before

the outbreak of war. The whole article illustrates his belief in the importance of national character as a vital factor in international relations. In the course of his article,
Ludwig asserted that:

> The man who regards raw materials as more important
> than a people's philosophy; or who believes that figures de-
> cide history and not feelings, is liable to be surprised by
> a sudden outburst of national character. . . .
> If before the [First World] war, the international secret
> services had busied themselves with other people's character
> instead of their guns, the Germans would have known what
> the Anglo-Saxon character means and would never have
> ventured on war. Today, if the Americans and the English
> would study German character, they might yet ward off
> the war which threatens. That is my reason for writing on
> this subject, which I studied for twenty years.
> The mystic bent in the German character is most danger-
> ous in politics. . . .

Ludwig, a scholar, historian, and life-long student of
European foreign relations, thus supports the contention
of this book, that it is just as important for foreign intelligence services to busy themselves with other people's
character as with their guns. In some cases, it can be
more important. Anyone who neglects national character
may be due for a rude surprise.

Example 3. The Projected Invasion of England in 1940

A vivid account of the projected German invasion of
England in the critical months after Dunkirk is given in
Fleming's *Operation Sea Lion* (68). This book describes
the situation both from the German and the British point
of view. It describes the civilian and political, as well as

the military aspects of the threatened invasion of Britain. Fleming has no axe to grind, nor any moral to draw. His sole purpose is to give a vivid, truthful, and well-balanced account of this dramatic episode in World War II.

Even if Fleming teaches no lesson, he clearly has his own point of view and basic assumptions, like all other historians. One of these—though it is not stated explicitly in so many words—is the necessity for understanding national character as a guide to foreign relations. Frequent references to this necessity occur in his pages: "The real, the ultimate reason why Hitler failed to invade England was because he failed to understand her." He says again: "He [Hitler] was not likely to be right about the [British] people, of whom he knew nothing at all."

It is Fleming's well-supported contention that it was Hitler's failure to understand the British character which led him to take exactly the wrong attitude toward the British on two or three critical occasions at this period. Once again, Hitler's intelligence regarding British economic and military establishments, though not of course perfect, was reasonably adequate. His intelligence regarding the British national character was fatally deficient.

To show how fundamental and all-pervading this idea is, in Fleming's definitive description of this crucial episode in World War II, suppose Fleming's publisher had said to him: "In a military situation it is hard facts like guns and ships and supplies that count. National character is an exploded idea. Stick to hard facts." An examination of the text shows that the concept of understanding national character could not have been eliminated with a blue pencil by crossing out certain words, sentences or even paragraphs. So basic is this concept to this book and by implication to the whole situation after Dunkirk that much of the book would need to be rewritten in order to eliminate the national character concept. Furthermore, no other concept could replace it as an adequate substitute.

Wheatley's book on the same subject (69), based on the original German documents, likewise makes frequent reference to Hitler's belief that the British would surrender without invasion. According to a German staff officer, "Hitler seriously expected the outbreak of a revolution in England."

Finally, Sir Winston!

Let us sum of with a phrase of Sir Winston Churchill. Speaking in December, 1941, shortly after Pearl Harbor, to the Congress of the United States about the Nazis, he said: "What kind of a people do they think we are?" Not, "How do they estimate our gross national product?"

Again consider Sir Winston's *History of the English-Speaking Peoples*. In the last volume, entitled *The Great Democracies*, and when answering the question regarding the secret of the spread of the English-speaking peoples over a quarter of the globe, he gives the answer: "Character, surmounting the strain and terror of an angry world by masterful energy." Again character predominates, even when "hard facts" alone might well point to conclusions quite different.

SUMMARY

What worthwhile contributions can be claimed for this study?

I believe we have made the following gains which improve our ability to understand foreign peoples and to apply the concept of national character to practical problems in foreign intelligence and foreign relations.

1. *Meanings.* We who are interested in this subject gain a clearer understanding of the meaning of the term national character and of related terms so often encountered in social science studies and in intelligence reading.

2. *Analogy with Personal Character.* We learn that national character is closely analogous to personal character. Many considerations pertaining to the study of personal character for use in dealings between individuals can be adapted to the study of national character for use in dealings between nations.

3. *Character-Forming Influences.* We find that the character of an individual is based upon his inborn characteristics as modified by his physical and cultural environment. In a group there is a mutual interaction between the character of the group and that of the individual within the group. In a nation there is a similar interaction

158

between the character of the nation and the characters of the individuals and of the groups within the nation.

Many of the strongest character-forming influences of environment—such as language, traditions, heroes, basic beliefs, mores, form of government, collective maturity— affect a large proportion of the individuals in each nation. These character-forming elements, which permeate the whole nation, naturally tend to give some elements of uniformity to the effective characters of the individuals, of the groups, and of the nation as a whole.

4. *Group Character.* We learn the mechanism by which groups serve as intermediaries between the individual and the nation; and how groups influence the character and actions of the nation as a whole. The study of group character proves to be particularly fruitful.

5. *Psychology and Social Sciences.* Although psychology and the social sciences form a useful background, yet the studies of individual psychology, social psychology and the related social sciences are at present *inadequate to serve as practical guides* for our judgments of individual or of national character. In looking for help from psychology and the social sciences, the intelligence or foreign service officer must exercise a high degree of critical selection. In addition he must use the other approaches which are here developed.

6. *National Character as a Major Factor.* We find that national character enters as a major factor in each of the recognized components of strategic intelligence, and so is a major factor in most international situations. The developments to be expected in the field covered by each component are largely indicated by the product: *Hard Facts x National Character.* To this may be added *x Situation* as a third factor to represent the favorable or unfavorable elements in the background situation. As two typical examples out of many:

For Military developments. Weapons x Character of
the People who will use the weapons;

For Political developments: Political Institutions x
Character of the People who must implement these
institutions.

National character is in danger of being neglected because it cannot be expressed as definitely as can the hard
facts, but it *must* be considered.

7. *Three Fruitful Fields.* Three aspects of national character were selected for emphasis. These are particularly
rewarding for *advanced study* by the intelligence or foreign service officer. The three fields are:

a) Basic Beliefs and Fundamental Philosophy.
b) Mechanism of the Action of Groups within a
Nation.
c) Critical Search for Indications of Impending
Change in Character.

8. *Differences between Nations Pertinent to National
Character.* Most nations will exhibit elements of individuality, and corresponding traits of national character
which will be characteristic of *each nation when acting as
a nation.* These differences in the characters of the nations
arise from the fact that most nations are significantly
different from all others in many of the following par-
ticulars:

a) The individual character of its people—all of whom
have been subjected to the over-all national character-
forming influences mentioned in Section 7.

b) The Basic Beliefs of the people as described in Section 6 are more or less different from that of other nations.

c) The inner characters of the influential groups

within the nation are different from those found elsewhere.

d) The mechanism of the action of the political, economic, religious, educational and other cultural groups within the nation is different from that of any other.

e) The geographic position, history, traditions, education, mores, political parties, and political institutions of one nation are characteristic of that nation.

f) The exports, imports, aspirations, fears, and foreign policy are significantly different from that of other nations.

With all of the above differences it is natural to expect and to find significant, knowable, and consistent differences in the national character of most nations.

9. *The Unique Role.* We end with some examples of the unique role of national character in strategic intelligence and foreign relations whereby this concept may lead us to *conclusions not indicated by any other approaches.*

10. *The Characters of Specific Nations.* A Supplement to the Bibliography lists books which give specific information regarding the characters of each of the leading nations.

CONCLUSIONS

1. National Character is closely analogous to personal character.

2. The character of a given nation is usually sufficiently consistent and knowable, so that its study will provide vitally helpful material for the production of an intelligence estimate or for dealings with that nation.

3. National character is of outstanding importance because it enters as one of the two or three major factors in *each* of the nine components of strategic intelligence and area studies.

4. A consideration of national character is an essential part of any international situation, because we can often obtain from such consideration vital conclusions which cannot be obtained in any other manner.

L'ENVOI

A Glance into the Future

It is a commonplace that we live in a world of change. Few fully realize how greatly the *rate of change* has increased. This accelerated rate of change will probably continue. Positive pressure for further changes will continue to be exerted by new discoveries and by past changes. Resistance to change will continue to be diminished by education, rapid communications, and the ease of transportation for goods and people.

In no field of human activities will change be more unprecedentedly rapid than in international relations. Since the end of World War II, we have witnessed radical changes in India, Burma, Pakistan, Ceylon, Indo-China, Indonesia, U.S.S.R. and all of the European satellites. At the present time rapid changes are occurring in most of Africa, the whole of the Middle East, much of the Far East, and elsewhere. Both the rapid increase in world population and the general increase in economic competition accompanied by the industrialization of backward countries will accelerate this landslide of change. The present explosive period in international relations will continue for several generations at least.

So in international affairs old assumptions are shifting. A constant reappraisal of all important factors, including the national character of those with whom we deal, will become necessary. A recognition of the importance of this last-named factor will increase. Reliance upon mental Maginot Lines will become more and more disastrous.

Due to the political, economic, and other changes mentioned, even more aggressive competition in the international field must be expected. It will be carried out in all of its aspects more and more by professionals with advanced training in the various fields, including the fields of foreign intelligence and national character.

As to progress in our comprehension of the concept of national character, we can expect that practical information will slowly increase, followed by a better understanding of basic principles and by the development of better methods. Some of the earliest definite evidences of progress will probably consist in the elimination of some current fallacies, and in the development of simpler methods for the study of the character of foreign peoples, and for the expression of the results in the language of the common man.

The *art* of understanding national character for practical purposes will probably remain in advance of the *science* of the determination of national character—just as the art of understanding personal character for practical human dealings has always been ahead of any scientific determination in this field.

Expert knowledge will be demanded to a much greater extent than at present, but experienced professional judgment will continue to be needed as much as ever. An understanding of national character and the spirit of the people will always be gained principally from personal contact, the methods of the social sciences, and human insight, rather than from those of mathematical statistics.

It is primarily a human problem.

SOME CHARACTERISTICS
OF NATIONS AND
SMALLER GROUPS

The diversity of the sovereign nations (which perfectionists like to call nation-states) actually existing on this globe is enormous. There are also aggregations of persons known as peoples, nationalities, etc., which are hopeful of becoming nations. Then the smaller aggregations, called groups in this book, may be called by any one of an extraordinary number of names, such as societies, communities, ethnic groups, etc.

The whole field of human organization presents a rich and rewarding field of study, the pursuit of which broadens one's comprehension of the diversity of ways in which human beings may be associated and the diversity of factors which may serve to hold them together in nations or groups, or to drive them apart.

An excellent and original discussion of nations and their component parts is that by Deutsch entitled *Nationalism and Social Communication, An Inquiry into the Foundations of Nationality* (46). Much of his book, as is evident from the title, is of interest to the student of national character.

The following definitions of nations and groups within a nation are taken from his book, directly or with some abbreviations. They are given generally in descending order of size and degree of autonomy. As we look them over we notice that each group here defined is associated with its own cluster of attributes—political, historical, economic, geographical, cultural, psychological. A consideration of the full meaning and limitations of each attribute adds to our understanding of the group in question. We speedily see that few groups possess all of the basic attributes usually considered typical for that kind of group. For example, a typical nation is generally considered to be continuous geographically as to the nation itself (without considering dependencies). Yet such is not the case with Pakistan, nor with the United States when we remember the new states of Alaska and Hawaii. In a nation we generally expect to find one dominant language, religion, climate, history, race, and various dominant elements of culture. Yet we find very many very important exceptions. So again we realize that in this field there are no definitive, rigorous definitions. Man has not organized himself in such logical and clean-cut units. It is *misleading to make our definitions more precise than the realities which they attempt to describe.* So instead of "definitions" it would be better to say: Here are a few rambling discussions, each of which will add to our understanding of what is meant in this book by each of the kinds of human associations named. There is no description here to which there are not plenty of exceptions. Each description is worthy of thought, as showing how many points of view and how many disciplines are involved in the make-up and operation of each kind of association of human beings. Therefore each description is enlightening;

but do not take any of them too seriously. There is much overlapping, and there are no sharp boundaries. Different writers, as is so common in the social sciences, may use any of these terms in a different meaning.

A Nation. "It seems . . . more fruitful . . . to define a nation as a people possessing national consciousness which . . . is also a matter of degree. . . . National consciousness consists in the combined striving for unity, liberty, individuality and prestige.[1] . . . The decisive criterion is whether the idea of a duty to sacrifice particular interests to the national has become dominant in the people." (71) Professor E. H. Carr summarized the position in 1945: "*The nation is not a definable and clearly recognizable entity* . . . it embodies in itself . . . such natural and universal elements as attachments to one's native land and speech and a sense of wider kinship than that of family. The modern nation is a historical group." (72) For a more hopeful reference Deutsch suggests that of Brinton (73, pp. 500-502).

It is further agreed by most serious writers that the idea of a nation "implied some similar elements inside the minds of every individual participating in it, such as common values, thoughts or feelings, . . . All these elements —relations to environment, past, leaders, institutions and symbols—were further shown as making up structures. . . . These high-order configurations of social behavior were called 'collective personalities' by some writers, and 'cultures' by others. . . . These social patterns then in turn were found to be related to the personality structure of individuals. Each individual's personality, and thus to some extent his nationality, were found to involve his 'consciousness' or 'will,' though . . . it was not settled to what extent they represented causes, and to what extent effects" (46, pp. 14-15).

A People. This term is loosely used for a group which

has much in common, but which is not a nation. As a rather vague definition, Deutsch (46) suggests "a people is a group of individuals who have some objective characteristics in common. These characteristics usually then are said to include language, territorial residence, traditions, habits, historical memories, and the like. To these are added . . . certain subjective elements such as mutual affection, consciousness of differences from other peoples, or the will to belong to this particular people." To most of us this definition will not add much that we do not already know.

A Nationality. This term is frequently encountered in the sense that a nation, such as Russia before 1917, contained several separate "nationalities," such as the Poles, Ukrainians, etc. According to Deutsch (46, pp. 3-4), "A nationality in this widespread usage is, then, a term which may be applied to a people among whom there exists a significant movement toward political, economic, or cultural autonomy, that is to say, toward a political organization, or a market area, or an area of literary or cultural interchange, within which the personnel and the characteristics of this people will predominate."

Deutsch (pp. 78-80) gives a description of the stages through which a nationality group, e.g., the Irish, existing as part of another nation must go to become an independent nation in its own right. This is summed up by the statement that "nationalities turn into nations when they acquire power to back up their aspirations."

A Community. Social scientists have used "community" in two quite different meanings. One meaning is a group of people living near to each other as in a small town, regardless of whether there is any sharing of ideas or feelings between the different parts. The second meaning of "community" and the one used by Deutsch is that of a group of people who share important elements of culture with one another; within such a group the communication is good.

Thus there can be communities of culture, of delusions, of government, of habits, of language, of values, national or territorial communities. Deutsch's use of "community" is much like the use of "group" in this book, namely, an association of people who have one or more interests in common which hold them together. Deutsch says:

> When we say "culture" we stress the habits, preferences and institutions as such, as if they were a configuration of disembodied ghosts. When we say "community" we stress the collection of living individuals in whose minds and memories the habits and channels of culture are carried.
>
> Both terms, then, have their distinct usefulness . . . nationality will be discussed in terms of community as here defined. But a great deal of valuable literature on peoples and nations has been written in terms of the culture concept. The overlapping relationship between the community and culture should be remembered. . . .

How Much Do Our Definitions Mean?

Deutsch brings out also the different meanings which may be attached to the various terms which are used as part of the descriptions of nations and groups. One characteristic which members of a nation are usually said to have in common is the fact that they all shall share a common and contiguous territory.

> In what sense is there a territorial community or contiguity between a German village on the Swiss border and a German village on the shores of the North Sea? In what sense does this contiguity differ from that with a Swiss village five miles across the political border? . . .
> The same difficulty of deciding just what makes a "com-

mon" condition or experience *effectively common* to a people applies to the community of history and memories. . . .

But *when* is a "common" heritage common? A recent investigator emphasizes the obvious fact that Europe is full of different nationalities who for centuries have been settled and intermingled in the same countries, such as Czechs and Germans in Bohemia. . . . their ancestors have lived through the same historic events in the same regions and yet there is no sharing: they continue to look upon these historical events from entirely different points of view. . . . To explain a nation as the result of shared experiences presupposes already this ability to share experience, which is the very thing that cannot be taken for granted.

Some other concepts which have from time to time been put forward as unifying influences are: a community of values; common sympathies.

Disraeli (74) said:

A nation is a work of art and a work of time. A nation is gradually created by a variety of influences—the influence of original organization, of climate, soil, religion, laws, customs, manners, extraordinary accidents and incidents in their history, and the individual character of their illustrious citizens. These *influences* create the nation—these *form the national mind.* . . .

If we say that members of a nation share a common culture, evidently a whole book could profitably be written about what is meant by "culture."

Deutsch continues later in his book:

It is now clear why all the usual descriptions of a people in terms of a community of languages, or character, or memories, or past history, are open to exception. For what counts is not the presence or absence of any single factor, but merely the presence of sufficient communication [2] facilities with enough complementarity to produce the over-all result. The Swiss may speak four different languages and still act as one people, for each of them has enough learned habits, preferences, symbols, memories . . . events in history, and personal associations, all of which together permit him to communicate more effectively with other Swiss than with the speakers of his own language who belong to other peoples.

Deutsch quotes Schuerch (75) along these lines as follows:

I found that my German was more closely akin to the French of my [French-Swiss] friend than to the likewise German of the foreigner. The French-Swiss and I were using different words for the same concepts, but we understand each other. The man from Vienna and I were using the same words for different concepts, and thus we did not understand each other in the least.

All of the above brings out two very practical lessons in the study of nations, nationalism, or national character. First, it illustrates again and again how diverse are the nations, peoples, societies, communities and other groups as they now actually exist on this earth. Second, it brings out that statements about nations and other subgroups and about cultures, communications, and related terms can never be swallowed whole even if they come from an undoubted authority in which we have every confidence. About every important term used we must ask ourselves: What does this man really mean by this term in this context? Also, over what range is any statement usually true; and even within this range, what are the chances of error or exceptions? Incidentally, this habit of being critical about the meaning and range and reliability of all statements made in the area of the social sciences, and especially in this field of foreign intelligence and foreign affairs, is a valuable habit to acquire. Without it, serious misunderstandings with the possibility of disastrous consequences are inevitable.

THE CAUSE AND/OR
EFFECT NETWORK

A group presents an excellent example of a situation which is common and important in the social sciences. In the examples described under the heading "Interactions of Individual and Group Character" in Section V which are typical, a member influences the group, and the group in turn influences the member, so that the feeling on a given subject builds up rapidly (a mathematician would say "exponentially"). This has been described as "reciprocal interaction rather than causation." So when we make a statement such as: "A feeling of optimism shown by some of the members strengthens the optimistic feeling of the group as a whole," we can usually add *and vice versa.* These words could in fact be meaningfully added to many of the statements of the present book.

This type of situation is important to understand, and is frequently encountered in the social sciences. As examples: (a) An educated society produces good educational institutions. But it is equally and *concurrently* true that (b) Good educational institutions produce an educated society. Again in a military situation: (a) Victories

173

are a cause of high morale. But also, (b) High morale is a cause of victories.

In philosophy, cause and effect are discussed. I have called the relationship here described, "Cause and/or Effect." Any given element may be considered as the cause and then considered as the effect. As a matter of fact, it acts *simultaneously* both as cause and effect.

The relationship may be expressed symbolically by the common chemical symbol of the two-way arrow indicating that a reaction goes both ways, namely $\rightleftharpoons$. The arrow may be read "brings about" and is read *both* from left to right *and* from right to left. Thus ill health $\rightleftharpoons$ low earnings.

This is a feed-back relationship. The principles involved have been set forth in discussions of logic and the scientific method (32).

So much for the effect of groups upon the character of their members (and vice versa) as an example.

The Cause and/or Effect relationship is so frequently found in the social sciences and is so fundamental in many of the operations by which human activities influence one another that it deserves discussion here. Anyone who gets a clear picture of this kind of relation will find that such knowledge clarifies his understanding of much of the inner workings of the formation and effects of national character, and that it helps to avoid many pitfalls in the interpretation of situations in this field.[1]

A fuller explanation of three terms, which are somewhat apart from one's usual thinking, will help to eliminate most of the difficulties. These terms, fundamental to an understanding of this subject, are:

A continuing process
Feedback
The Interdetermination Network

An attempt will be made here to present very briefly the high spots of an evolutionary situation which is subject to what has been called the Principle of Interdetermination.

Irrevocable—Instantaneous—Complete

As an introduction let us consider a single-action pistol with a hair trigger. The pistol is cocked and is loaded with a cartridge. Now if we pull the trigger, the hammer is released and falls on the firing pin. This sets off the powder in the cartridge which expels the bullet.

This is a simple train of cause and effect events of the kind that our minds like to dwell upon, because such events are clear-cut and simple. For the purposes of this elementary discussion the pulling of the trigger is irrevocable, instantaneous and complete. Once pulled it cannot be unpulled. It is essentially instantaneous, in that there is no time to modify its action. It is complete. It is never more pulled or less pulled. It is pulled, or it is not.

Many actions are of this kind. At a given moment in a game of cards the ace has either been played or it has not been played. It is never partly played. Once played the act is irrevocable. We can call such an action an *event*. In the case of an irrevocable, instantaneous and complete event, there is no feedback effect. Whether the cartridge fires or is a dud has no effect whatever on the trigger.

Consider now by contrast the firing of a one-minute burst of fire on a machine gun. The machine gun is designed so that the firing of a cartridge activates a recoil mechanism which expels the old shell, loads the gun with a fresh cartridge, and then fires the fresh cartridge. This continues as long as the trigger is held back. Here the one-minute burst of fire, taken as a whole, is a continuous *process*, in which the first fall of the hammer fires a cartridge. The firing of this cartridge causes the hammer to fall on the second cartridge. Any part of this cycle is both a cause and an effect in this *process*. The burst of fire is governed by one kind of feedback action by which the results of the first part affect the later part of the process.

A more instructive analogy for our present purposes is the "governor" on some types of engine. By this mechanism, when the engine begins to go too fast the amount of fuel fed to the engine is automatically cut down so that the engine goes more slowly. Likewise if the engine goes too slowly, the amount of fuel is automatically increased.

Such a process wherein feedback action is possible, is evidently in sharp contrast to an irrevocable, instantaneous and complete event. It is not irrevocable because once the engine is started it may be stopped. It is not instantaneous. It is not complete. It can be run faster or slower. It is, in fact, subject to feedback or other guidance.

Feedback

The above gives a simple example of the feedback mechanism by which a process in nature or human actions is subject to automatic control or guidance through some mechanism built into the process itself.

For example, in an isolated community the number of wild animals of a given species regulates itself. If more are born than the territory can support they die of disease or starvation. If too few are born, the death rate drops.

The feedback can do more than say Go or Stop to a process; it can act as a means of effective guidance throughout a complicated process. A detailed description of such feedback *guidance* for a problem in intelligence production is given with charts in my book on *Strategic*

Intelligence Production (38, pages 75-88). It is directly pertinent to the present discussion.

A clear-cut application of this point of view is given by national character. The character of a given nation is not a fixed event. It is the end product of a very complicated *process*. Character is not provided ready-made; it is provided by character-forming influences. As these influences change, so the character slowly changes. Even if the character should remain the same (which it does not), the outward effects of the character would change as a result of other changes in the domestic or international situation.

Evidently I am not offering the reader a lazy man's program for understanding or dealing with international situations. I believe that the picture which we draw faithfully represents the actual situation, within the limits implicit in a picture of this nature. I believe further that this approach is practical and offers the best chances for success in the task which we have set before ourselves. This task is the acquisition of a sound understanding of foreign countries, and the production of foreign intelligence of the highest quality.

But worse is to follow.

The Interdetermination Network

Let us start again with a simple analogy from the physical world, say the forces which influence the flight of a 90-mm artillery projectile. Taking the principal forces, we may say that they are the force of gravity, the action of the explosive giving to the projectile a muzzle velocity in the direction of the angle of fire, the resistance of the air, the effect of wind, and the effect of the spin. It is evident that some forces pull the projectile down toward the earth; others force it upward; some, like windage, may force it sideways. By the relatively simple mathematics of elementary ballistics we can calculate the *net effect* of all of these forces which sometimes work wholly or partially at cross purposes. For practical calculations we can regard these forces as independent of one another. For example, the force of gravity acts on the projectile. We do not have to consider that the force of gravity also acts on the air resistance, or that these two react to increase or decrease the force of gravity (which they do not).

In human relations as depicted by the social sciences and as exemplified in international relations including the effects of national character, there are many forces which influence a given situation. However, in the social sciences, unlike physics, there is no formula by which we can calculate the net effect of these forces. These forces act as causes, which result in certain effects observable in human behavior. Furthermore, these social forces are *not independent*. They have an interaction upon one another. To make matters still worse, in the continuing process which is a social reaction, the same force may be both a cause and an effect.

This situation is summed up by Lasswell and Kaplan (27, page XVII) as follows:

> In particular, full emphasis is given to the multiplicity of factors involved in any given political event—an emphasis that may be designated as a *principle of interdetermination.* This standpoint is sometimes formulated as a principle of "multiple causation." But more is involved than multiple causes; there are multiple effects as well, and more important, there are patterns of interaction in which it is impossible to distinguish between cause and effect. Hence we speak of the interdetermination of a set of variables—each is correlated with the others. . . .
>
> The interdetermination of social variables is sometimes

taken as ground for denying the possibility of any social science: human affairs, it is urged, are too complex to lend themselves to theoretical simplifications. But the complex factors determining voting behavior, for instance, do not prevent us from making reliable election forecasts. And as Hume somewhere observes, we can be as certain that a bag of gold placed on Piccadilly Circus at noon will have disappeared at 1 P.M. as if it had been a block of ice.[2]

A "Conceptual Model"

Imagine a group of ten small fishing boats anchored closely around a spot in a quiet arm of the sea. A fisherman in one of the boats hooks a large fish. He starts to reel it in. The fish does not resist. The pull of the line and the resistance of the water to the movement of the fish represent a simple case of cause and effect respectively. Now suppose that by chance one fisherman from each of the other boats hooks this same fish at the same time. Each pulls in a different direction. Here we have ten independent causes (multiple causation). Now suppose that the action of each fisherman influences each of the others. Some are irritated so that they pull harder than ever on their own lines. Some slacken up in an effort to be co-operative. In that case the action of each would have a secondary action on the others. Here we have forces which have become *interdependent*. Also many fishermen are acting as both a cause and effect. Now suppose that other fishermen in the boats cast their lines out toward the fish thereby crossing their lines with those of the first fishermen, snarling them up crosswise, and forming in effect an irregular *network* with each force influencing many others.

At this point the large fish becomes sporadically very active. He is so large and strong that he pulls the fishing boats toward him at some moments. By so doing the fish becomes not only an effect to be pulled in, but also a cause which does some of its own pulling. The action of the fish exhibits the principle of interdetermination on each of the fishermen in a different way. Some are stimulated to greater activity; others are scared, or discouraged.

At this time a strong tide starts running out to sea, superimposing this over-all force on the whole situation. A high wind rises and produces choppy waves.

Here we have a faithful representation of the familiar principle of cause and effect complicated by becoming a case of cause and/or effect, and by multiple causes and multiple effects, all interacting with one another. The fish under study, instead of being pulled by one or a few fish lines, is tangled in *an irregular network* of fish lines (representing social forces) *all interconnected.*

Many scholars have discussed the formulation of a "conceptual model" of some social science situation to be studied. Deutsch (46, p. 60) says, for example:

> To seek understanding means to seek a conceptual model. . . . We seek a model which will fit the known facts. . . . More than that we want it to suggest new questions. . . . Each concept should be operational. . . .

Unfortunately most of these "models" turn out to be mathematical equations (46, Appendix V). The fisherman's model presented above can be defended by some of the standards just quoted. It "fits the known facts," "suggests new questions" (for example, Did they land the fish?) and is certainly "operational." Perhaps it is just as "conceptual" as some formulas from higher mathematics.

Speaking now more seriously, I believe the picture of a

network of many interrelated forces, each one a cause and/or effect, is sound, and fruitful, and about as near as one can come to a physical picture of the "pulling and hauling" of conflicting human interests. In this network, however, some few strands are actually very strong. They represent the controlling factors. Some strands are weak. Many of these weaker strands can be tentatively disregarded. All, however, are interconnected. It *is* possible to find some guiding principles.

A foreign service officer or a foreign intelligence officer must recognize that his problems are at least as complicated as the problems here described.

WHAT ONE FACTOR
GOVERNS AN
INTERNATIONAL SITUATION?

There is always an intriguing, but completely futile, argument, as to whether great men cause great events or whether a great event would happen anyway, so that the event merely gives an opportunity for some man to achieve greatness by appearing to lead it. This is the old question discussed by Carlyle in *On Heroes, Hero-Worship, and the Heroic in History.*

This idea is sometimes stated as: "Events, not men, shape the big decisions." Mills (76) puts it: Those who say this "are echoing the theory of history as Fortune, Chance, Fate, or the work of the Unseen Hand. For events are merely a modern word for these older ideas all of which separate men from history-making, because all of them lead us to believe that history goes on behind men's backs."

When anyone, in discussing the controlling factors in the actions of peoples in the past (history) or in the future (intelligence estimates), pretends that there is any *one* factor which is overwhelmingly important—so that all others occupy only minor roles—heed him not. Arguments implying a dichotomy—Is it this or that?—are also generally misleading.

As a warning consider the following examples, all stated in simplified terms:

1. Is the course of history—past or future—controlled by great men, or by the character of the people with whom the great men must work?

The simple answer is that consideration of *both* is necessary and important for a correct understanding of the situation. (Hence the significance of national character.)

2. In historical writing, which is the more important—detailed historical accuracy resulting from scholarly research, or a vivid, colorful, lifelike historical presentation?

The simple answer is *both* are necessary and important. Yet thousands of man-hours have been wasted in arguing this point. As one example, see Trevelyan (77).

Some individual historians have more talent in historical research, others in lively description. History as a profession has responsibility for providing the public with both aspects of the truth. The same statement may be made regarding the intelligence profession and those working in the field of international relations.

3. Is the economic problem the basic controlling factor in most situations, even those which superficially seem to be in other fields (such as the Protestant Reformation or the American Revolution)?

The simple answer is *no*.

The economic situation is nearly always important, but it can never be more than a part of the picture. See Beard (47), quoted in (27), p. 94n.

This has been summed up by Lasswell and Kaplan as follows:

While there may be similarities of "motive, passion and desire" among various persons and cultures, there are differences as well, differences especially in the comparative importance attached to the various values. . . .

In particular, it is impossible to assign a universally dominant role to some one value or other. No single principle of motivation can be elaborated into a tenable "philosophy of history"—as though always and everywhere human conduct can be interpreted as striving only for economic gain, or for political power, or for prestige and glory, or for love and affection. In a specific situation, any or all of these—and others as well—might be involved in different degrees. What values are operative, and to what extent, can be determined only by specific empirical inquiry (27, pp. 56-7).

The last sentence leaves plenty of work in the form of specific empirical inquiries still to be done by the intelligence officer or foreign service officer.

SHORTCOMINGS OF
EARLIER SCIENTIFIC WORK

Present Research Methods

In *Tensions Affecting International Understanding* (13) Klineberg gives a critical survey of the researches into methods for the determination of differences in national character. This is discussed under the following headings (emphasis has been added) which are reproduced here so as to give some idea of the many approaches to this subject:

Descriptive Accounts
Descriptions and Interpretations by Anthropologists
Vital and Social Statistics
Psychiatric Interpretations
Psychoanalytic and Modified Psychoanalytic
   Approaches
Psychosomatic Relationships
Content Analysis of Cultural Products
Community Studies
Public Opinion Surveys
Attitude Studies

Intensive Interviews
Tests and Measurements
The Semantic Approach
Child Training

I am impressed with the tremendous amount of careful and thoughtful work which has been done. I am also impressed with the present shortcomings of each of the methods discussed. I concur with the following extracts from the conclusion to this part of Klineberg's study:

> The fact that such a large variety of techniques has been distinguished in this field of study in itself indicates that no one technique has as yet been judged completely satisfactory. The problem of "national character" or of personality in relation to nationality is exceedingly complex.
>
> The various techniques all suffer from the same defect, namely that their validity has never been fully established.
>
> At the present time there seems to be only one adequate method of determining the validity of these techniques, and that is by a combined approach. . . .
>
> Whatever their origins, the characteristic patterns of behavior do differ, and we need to know as precisely as possible how they differ. . . .

See also Klineberg's very readable summary of the present status of scientific research on national character in his *Social Psychology* (18), pages 377 to 393 and in his *A Science of National Character* (78).

Sources of Practical Information

To these conclusions I would add three conclusions of my own. These three are closely connected with the purpose of the present book, which is the *practical utilization of the knowledge of national character* in

foreign intelligence and in foreign relations. These conclusions are:

1. The various approaches described above for what
may be called "scientific methods" to the determination
of national character are still so far short of their goal
that many of them are profitable fields of study only
by those whose primary interest is academic, and not
those whose primary interest is the practical solution of
some current problem of foreign intelligence or foreign
relations.

In other words, under present conditions these methods
are profitable for study by those who are primarily anthropologists, psychologists, psychiatrists, etc., but not yet
practically profitable for study by those who are primarily
foreign intelligence officers, foreign service officers, or
by those who, without being specialists in any part of
this field, are interested in understanding current problems in international relations. In fact the claims made
for *some* of these methods are not only confusing, they
seem to me actively misleading. See *Sense and Nonsense
in Psychology* (79).

2. Most of the ideas for the *practical application* of
personal character and national character in personal
and national relations, respectively, will come at the
present time from history, the social sciences, area studies,
the principles of intelligence, experience, and common
sense, all digested by mature thought, and refined by
critical examination. The accepted principles of elementary psychology are well established and reliable. To
go beyond this under "psy-" in the dictionary is not now
practically profitable.

For the present we must continue to lean heavily on
the judgment of a knowledgeable and experienced person
rather than on formulas. Suggestions for gaining the
necessary knowledge and acquiring such judgment are

given in this text and in the references listed in the Bibliography.

3. In the United States government we should put more emphasis on getting information and in utilizing mature judgment regarding national character from those in the foreign service and others *who have lived in the countries* concerned. Such people should be made much more easily available for informal discussions at the working level to assist in the production of foreign intelligence and in the formulation and implementation of foreign policy. The knowledge which such people *can* get of the character of the nation to which they are accredited, is roughly similar to the knowledge of personal character which one gets of another person, not by studying records, but by personal contacts. There is no substitute for it.

National Stereotypes—Importance and Dangers

A study of national stereotypes shows that they are unexpectedly important, misleading, and dangerous.

By stereotypes I mean such figures as the Jew as represented by Shylock, the Irishman (usually named Pat) in the after-dinner stories, the stage Englishman, the stock characters in fiction representing other nationalities. The stereotype idea is perpetuated by phrases and clichés such as "the unspeakable Turk." We may mean by national stereotype also the way in which the representatives of each race or nation are commonly depicted in the newspapers, magazines, movies, books (including textbooks) and other mass media of a given country. Extensive checks of the mass media of one nation often bring out consistent patterns of favorable or unfavorable reference in regard to certain other nations.

A distinction must be made between the national

stereotypes exhibited by mass media, and the stereotypes exhibited by the private opinions of individuals. Though these are closely related, they are not the same.

One common source of error which may occur when we allow a stereotype to influence our thinking and our judgment in a specific instance is that the *particular* Jew, or Irishman, or Arab in question at the time of our decision may have none of the characteristics of the stereotype of his group.

In my opinion, national or racial stereotypes often have a rational basis and contain a kernel of truth, although never the whole truth. On the other hand, it is easy to demonstrate that many have an inadequate basis in fact, and some no factual basis at all. They are unreliable, usually prejudicial, hence dangerous. The danger is reduced if people are made aware of the error involved. We would all agree that misinformation is not a basis upon which to build international understanding.

For much of the above I am indebted to the long and interesting chapter on national stereotypes in Klineberg's excellent survey of research on international understanding (13).

NOTES

Notes to Preface

1. This book is my second of a trilogy on subjects related to foreign intelligence production. These three books will bracket, but certainly cannot pretend to cover, this subject. The trilogy consists of:

Strategic Intelligence Production—Basic Principles (38). This is elementary and basic. It includes "The Nine Principles of Intelligence." One of these principles is national character, there called "the spirit of the people."

The present volume is a study of the practical applications of national character in intelligence and foreign relations. It is an illustration of how one of the nine principles may be usefully developed and applied.

The third volume, *Guidance from Uncertain Evidence—A Program for Progress in Intelligence and Foreign Relations,* will be an advanced study of principles and methods making maximum use of logic, probability and what may be called "Homodynamics."

Notes to Section 1

1. In *Strategic Intelligence Production—Basic Principles* (38) I comment on the shortcomings of the training in intelligence production, and the deficiencies of intelligence production as a professional career. Since 1957 little improvement has been made along these lines.

190

2. Besides the daily papers, see, for example, *The State Department and the Foreign Service* (1A); *Diplomat* (2); the fifteen reports as parts of *Study of United States Foreign Policy* made to U.S. Senate Foreign Relations Committee 1959 to 1960 (3); *The Mid-Century Challenge to U.S. Foreign Policy* (4); *What's Wrong with U.S. Foreign Policy* (5); *The Ugly American* (6); Northrop (43A) Chapters 2 and 6; and *Diplomacy in a Changing World* (7). Many of the shortcomings brought out in *The Ugly American* are the same as those emphasized in this book.

3. As examples, we find that very experienced members of the U.S. Foreign Service and Intelligence Community may differ on the meaning of "foreign intelligence." This is shown later in the present Introduction. On words as common and fundamental as "capabilities" persons as senior and as able as a Secretary of Defense or a Chief of Naval Operations may stumble badly. (See my *Strategic Intelligence Production—Basic Principles*, page 67. See also *N. Y. Times*, Jan. 26, 1960, page 1, col. 5.) It is high time that the Department of State, the Department of Defense and the whole Intelligence Community should regularly define much more clearly than they now do their important terms. This precaution is still neglected at all levels from the Joint Chiefs of Staff level down —with unfortunate results.

4. The Intelligence Community and others concerned with foreign relations and national security make a clear distinction between information and intelligence. *Information,* often pointedly referred to as "mere information," is a collection of raw data. Intelligence is the meaningful picture formed by putting these data together so that their relation and significance is indicated. As a simple example, the number of freight cars loaded with ammunition moving toward a given combat area averaged one a day for twenty days, then jumped to ten a day for a week. That is raw information. Anyone who can see and can count can collect it. These bare facts lead us to look for other bits of raw information. When put together, all these bits of raw information—no one of which means much alone—lead us to the conclusion that the enemy is planning to attack in that area. This meaningful statement is intelligence.

Holt and van de Welde illustrate this difference in a slightly different context when they say: "Information personnel are newshawks; they must be alert, observant and quick. . . . They must anticipate and report events, but need not really think about the meaning of them. The intelligence people, on the other hand, should be considerably less news-conscious and far more conscious of the meaning behind the news. *They are interpretive columnists rather than reporters."* (Emphasis added.)

Intelligence operations are divided into (1) field collection, (2) intelligence production, which is putting the information together so that it forms a meaningful picture, and (3) dissemination to those concerned.

5. Some have objected to striving for a "sympathetic understanding" of a potential enemy as being perhaps a contradiction in terms or an evidence of careless phraseology. I feel strongly that the acquisition of a sympathetic understanding of the nation with which one is dealing is an asset of the greatest value to a foreign intelligence officer or to a foreign service officer.

Very briefly the case is as follows: Much of great value has been written about "putting ourselves mentally in another man's place." This can be accomplished in large part by some people, and very little by others. To the extent that it is possible, it guides us in every aspect of foreign relations. To some extent we can understand what arguments, or pressures, or inducements will appeal to the foreign representatives with whom we are dealing. It gives us a better chance to outthink them and outmaneuver them. This operation is technically called *verstehen* (8A).

To acquire the ability in foreign intelligence or foreign relations even partially to think like a Communist is to have the ability to go into the contest well-prepared. We minimize the chance of being taken by surprise. We foresee probable developments.

To be able to think like a Communist does not mean that a person is "pink" *to the slightest degree.* On the contrary, it helps us to be one jump ahead of the Communist. So do not waste your time hating your enemy. You can do him much more damage if you first *understand* him. The most complete understanding is a sympathetic understanding.

This definition differs from those commonly accepted. Differences are: First, in emphasizing *understanding* as the central purpose of foreign intelligence; second, in bringing out the fact that most intelligence has no hostile implication whatever, but is aimed at mutual understanding between nations; finally, in pointing out the outstanding importance of obtaining reliable current intelligence about neutrals and ostensible friends as well as about nations known to be unfriendly.

The recent progress of events has justified and emphasized the point of view presented in this definition. Less than ten years ago the opinion prevailing in the U.S. Government was that nearly all of our intelligence attention should be focused on the Communist countries. Efforts spent on intelligence and in understanding neutrals and countries known to be friendly was considered largely a waste of time. What could be more trivial for example than devoting real talent to a country so well-known as Cuba? It should now be evident that we cannot afford to have second-rate representatives even in neutral or friendly countries, or second-rate men in Washington interpreting intelligence.

Notes to Section 2

1. This inner, deeper, stable aspect of character is a very real and important attribute, but it cannot be fully expressed in any one word. The idea is best conveyed by a consideration of several statements. For example:

"Character might almost be defined as the individual's system or complex of values." See Potter (20).

"In order that any society may function well, its members must acquire the kind of character which makes them *want* to act in the way that they *have* to act as members of that society or of a special class within it. They have to *desire* what objectively is necessary for them to do. *Outer force* is to be replaced by *inner* compulsion, and by the particular kind of human energy which is channeled into character traits." Eric Fromm, "Individual and Social Origins of Neurosis" in Kluckhohn and Murray (21), p. 517.

2. Ginsberg supports this meaning when he says: "The study of national character is to be approached *not* through an investigation of individual differences in behavior, but of the qualities manifested in the collective life of nations, their traditions and public policy" (16). This last clause forms a good definition of the national character of a nation when acting as a nation. This aspect of national character has been somewhat neglected.

Notes to Section 3

1. The part here italicized constitutes the present author's informal, nontechnical, but *operational* working definition of personal character.

2. Mark Twain says (truthfully) in his autobiography (17) that he found within himself the same traits of character as those found in George Washington—but present to a different degree.

3. Exceptions are, of course, some traits of character which would not become manifest in an office, such as physical courage and those traits shown only in family relationships. There are also the *very* rare cases of the tried and true employee who turns out to be an embezzler.

Notes to Section 4

1. For the past decade few writers who made any pretensions to high standards of scholarship have been willing to present a *simplified* description of anything without calling it *over*simplified. The plainer term is now hardly ever used. In contrast to such scholarly scholars, I claim that the present statement is simplified to the degree best suited to the objectives of this book. If it has a fault, it lies in the direction of being *under*simplified.

2. For excellent scientific statements of inborn qualities see P. B. Medawar, *The Uniqueness of the Individual* (21A) and *The Future of Man* (21B). From the former we learn that each individual is even more unique than we had previously believed. I use the outlawed phrase "more unique" advisedly.

3. It could almost be said that the meaning of culture always seems to be getting broader and broader. In this it perhaps resembles the equally disturbing concept of the ever-expanding universe.

Notes to Section 5

1. In this short lecture by Sir Harold Nicolson delivered in 1938, he includes excellent sketches of the characters of the British, Germans, Russians, Americans and Greeks.

2. The Establishment, according to Drew Middleton (53), "is an amorphous association of political, administrative, educational, economic and religious interests that operates the summit of British society. It epitomizes the Labor party's image of a reactionary ruling class united by education, business, social and marriage links and opposed to democratic progress."

I should modify this statement by saying that the Establishment includes the classes named when at the summit and *also* when on their way up. This is a completely informal and unofficial group. It has a side very beneficial to the efficiency of government.

Acquaintance with others in the Establishment has helped many members in the British government service to perform their duties better on account of the friendly and proper co-operation that they receive from their colleagues, who are often previous acquaintances. On the other hand, this gives members a considerable personal advantage over those who are not members. It is criticized quite hostilely by Hugh Thomas (33). However, a reviewer in the *Times Literary Supplement* of October 16, 1959, says with some justice the Establishment could be assumed to mean "people holding important jobs who throughout history have irritated young men in a hurry and older men who have missed the boat." It is a typical example of the working of results which arise out of the British national character.

3. Key (35) was able to write a large book on *Politics, Parties and Pressure Groups* without using the word "elite" at all. Certainly this word does not appear in the index, and apparently nowhere in the body of the book. To write a book on this subject without elite in 1958 was a real achievement. Of course he used "leadership" to include leaders proper, and also the elite concept as was generally done by earlier writers before the word became so fashionable and so enviable.

4. Some descriptions such as Mills's *The Power Elite* (76), leave the impression that the existence of an elite is somehow undesirable, undemocratic, or unfair. It seems to me that this is not necessarily the case. Let us take the guidance of a ship, the administration of a corporation, or the command of a military unit as examples. It seems that in each case it is desirable to have the administration and control concentrated in a few hands, except as to broad principles of general policy. Take the pilot of a ship, as a simplified example of all other cases. It seems desirable that he should have every privilege and facility for performing his

function under the most favorable conditions, such as a good pilot house, good communications, authority, and good pay.

The "democracy" and "fairness" depend upon the means by which an elite is recruited. If promotion is by merit and open to all who can demonstrate ability to do the successive jobs on the way up, then it may be both democratic and fair. Such a process is healthy because it tends to keep the organization in question responsive to changing conditions. It permits the infusion of new blood and new ideas.

In fact one cannot imagine how the affairs of a large corporation, or a large government department, or a military unit, for example, could have the benefit of foresight and initiative, and could be efficiently directed and administered, except through a small group of men specially selected for the purpose and given sufficient authority to carry out their responsibilities.

The dangers are: (a) The elite may give priority to serving their own interests rather than the interests of those whom they represent; (b) they may be overpaid for their services; (c) selection for membership in the elite may not be by merit, but may be restricted to certain families, to the upper classes, or to a self-perpetuating interlocking body of men, all in accordance with the picture drawn by Mills. For a description of a closely knit elite, see *The Establishment,* edited by Hugh Thomas (33).

5. Confirmations of this interesting statement are seen in the so-called civilian control of various technical services in the United States and Britain. For example, in the U.S., the Secretary of the Army, and in Britain the Secretary of State for War, are *politicians.* They are not highly skilled in military matters. Initially they may know almost nothing about them. Their mission is different. Their mission requires that they be experts in the political arts of dealing with men. They can leave military skills to their military advisers.

6. For estimating action in the more distant future, it is often necessary to consider a third factor, namely, the possible effect of an actively dissatisfied minority within the group. Such rebellious, often radical, minorities are frequently overlooked. In the recent past they have sometimes achieved surprising results in the overthrow of an apparently well-entrenched "old regime" in groups of many kinds. (See Section 7.)

7. This provides an excellent example of the central theme of this book, namely *national character as one important factor in any international situation, constantly interacting with other im-*

portant factors. The results of these interactions govern the final outcome. This interplay demonstrates again both the strength and the weakness of the national character concept as a tool in foreign intelligence production, or in understanding an international situation. It is a highly significant concept, in that it enters as one of the principal factors in almost every international problem, whether economic, political, military or other. If you omit a consideration of the *character of the people,* you leave out half of the picture. On the other hand, it *is never more than a part of the picture.* By itself it never provides the answer to your problem. The final outcome is always the result of the interaction of the character factor with other factors. To make a reliable estimate of the results of these interactions, the analyst or the team of experts or the foreign service officer must have a knowledge of one or more of the social sciences and a real understanding of the mechanisms and motivations in economic, political, military and other situations, and in many kinds of countries (including even those barbarous nations which do not have the advantage of an Anglo-Saxon point of view). Our foreign intelligence and our foreign policy often demonstrate the effect of our serious shortcomings in training along these lines.

8. Lasswell and Kaplan (27, pp. 152-161) have an interesting discussion of leaders and leadership. In this they call attention to a suggestive distinction which has been made between three types of leaders called "crowd compellers," "crowd exponents," and "crowd representatives." The first, men of the type of Alexander and Napoleon, are described as "men who can conceive of an idea, mold a crowd big enough to carry it into effect, and force the crowd to do it." The crowd exponents are those whose special skills lie in being able "to render articulate what is only vaguely or dimly felt or thought by the mass." The crowd representatives are leaders "who only express the known and settled opinion of the crowd." The quotations are from Conway (37), *The Crowd in Peace and War.*

9. This is a convenient fiction. Conditions never are equal of course. We really mean that some important factors are *very roughly equal* within a large margin of error, and as far as we can see. Even then we can never take this phrase too seriously.

10. In my *Strategic Intelligence Production—Basic Principles* (pp. 189-191) I point out the practical value of considering any aggregation of values as extending over a *range of values,* so that

the *distribution*, let us say the percentage, of those who have a given trait of character to a high, moderate or low degree, is of great practical importance. These percentages can seldom be measured, but they can often profitably be estimated with sufficient accuracy. In all of the social sciences, dealing as they do with the infinite variety of all qualities which may be encountered in human beings, it is valuable to be "probability-minded" and "distribution-minded." By this means we remember that in any random group of human beings we can expect to find a *distribution*, for example, of rich, average and poor; smart, ordinary and dull; high, medium and low in every human quality.

11. The percentages used in this discussion are hypothetical, and may vary widely. They are used to show only the general ranges of character which seem to exist as here loosely defined.

Notes to Section 6

1. These two terms are used here interchangeably. They may be conveniently abbreviated as BB or FF, or even as PP (primitive postulates).

2. Quoted from Ruth Benedict, *The Chrysanthemum and the Sword* (41), page 16.

3. *Ibid.*, p. 17.

4. Clyde Kluckhohn (40).

5. The Advisory Commission on Information (15) says of the USIA: ". . . it is evident that many officers going to the field lack sufficient knowledge of the area (including the psychology of the people) to which they have been assigned."

6. Benedict, *op. cit.*, p. 12.

7. Justice William O. Douglas (41A) constantly speaks of "the spirit of liberty" in the American people as being an essential factor in preserving our rights.

8. Northrop (43A) elaborates the essential nature of this point, and also our present shortcomings. He says (pages 23 and 88): "What must be avoided by any topmost policy maker or any of his diplomats is the confusion of one's own personal political, religious or secular convictions with those of the living law customs and positive political ideals of either one's own nation or the nation with which one is negotiating. . . . The unfortunate fact is that politicians, laymen and many social scientists corrupt their

descriptive judgments because their descriptive method is so intuitive and nebulous that they surreptitiously and frequently quite unconsciously smuggle in evaluative judgments of their own political party or nation or school of 'social science' when they are purporting merely to be describing another party or nation."

In this book (43A) Northrop makes a clear and essential distinction between the descriptive method and the evaluative method of reporting political or foreign intelligence (his Chapters 6 and 7). All of this is directly pertinent to the application of the concept of national character in foreign intelligence.

Notes to Section 7

1. "Mechanism" is used frequently for convenience in this book where the meaning is really "mode of operation." We do *not* mean here the kind of mechanism which is found in a machine where the working is exact and the results are predictable. For example, when gear A is turned at 10 rpm, it will always mesh with gear B and force the latter to turn at exactly 20 rpm. By contrast in the "mechanism" by which Pressure Group A influences Senator B, the result is by no means exact or predictable. Into the human reaction there is injected human hopes and fears, ambitions and jealousies, governed by a mixture of knowledge, prejudice and ignorance. Yet in both the machine and the human contacts, it is a meaningful expression to say that there is a mechanism by which one unit exerts pressure upon another. Let us not attempt to apply the original meaning too strictly. Such is in fact a common and highly disastrous failing of the social sciences, wherein they borrow terms like "force," "energy," "pressure," and then use these physical terms as though they had in the social sciences their same exactness of meaning.

2. As Ginsberg (16, p. 157) says, "Clearly there must be an intimate relation between the collective achievements of a people and the character of its components."

3. A defense of "pressure groups" was published in July, 1959, as a 54-page booklet entitled "Major Economic Groups and National Policy." This was the outcome of the tenth session of the American Round Table in Chicago sponsored by the University of Chicago and the Advertising Council. Among other things it points out that most of the interest groups give their views openly and frankly

to Congress. According to the report in *New York Times* of July 12, 1959, "Pressure groups are an integral part of American life and one of the significant developments of the twentieth century. . . . They may not always serve the public interest; sometimes they may harm it. On the whole, however, their activity does serve the public interest."

An excellent and detailed description of the activities of specific pressure groups is given by Key (35, pp. 24-177). The groups which he singles out for special emphasis are: agrarian, labor, business, veterans, religious, professional, and those having some foreign national origin such as the Irish, Zionists, German, Italian, Polish, etc.

4. The situation here described is common in nations which have the *forms* of parliamentary government, but not the national character (including traits of patriotism, self-restraint and good will) to make it work. See, for example, Mack Smith's *Italy: A Modern History* (49). This book is reviewed by Lowry Nelson (50), using "A Shortage of Heroes" as the expressive title of the review. The reviewer mentions the long succession of various coalitions of the smaller parties, accompanied by no consistent and coherent "loyal opposition." He says: "Though short on heroes, united Italy can count among its leaders many mediocrities, a number of pomposities, and one unredeemable villain" (Mussolini). The situation and the results are typical for nations which have the character of modern Italy, but which lack a dictator.

5. A discussion of influences which favor the establishment and maintenance of the two-party system in contrast to the multiparty system is given by Key (35), pp. 227-231.

6. In the case of political institutions it is evident that the hard facts regarding the quality of these institutions are not as "hard" as those for weapons or raw materials. That is, they cannot be expressed exactly in numbers of planes or tons of ore. Yet the basic approach is still sound.

7. Justice William O. Douglas makes this same point with the same example in the chapter on "The Bill of Rights in Action" in his book, *A Living Bill of Rights* (41A).

8. Lasswell and Kaplan (p. XXI) refer to this as the *principle of situational reference*. This is merely an abstract way of saying that in the social sciences few statements can safely be generalized and taken out of context. Most statements are more reliable and meaningful and convincing when the important factors in the general situation are clearly indicated as a context.

9. See for example: Lindzey, Gardner (Ed.), *Handbook of Social Psychology* (51A).

Notes to Section 8

1. *Punch* says: What is the difference between a Strong Man and a dictator? Answer. A Strong Man is a dictator who is, or is supposed to be, on Our Side. (Quotation from memory. Capitalization as in original.)

Notes to Section 9

1. I take British character as an illustrative example for convenience and because there is an abundance of good material on the British. It is easy to understand; it is easy to check by firsthand observation; there is no Iron Curtain.

Notes to Section 10

1. The present section is a defense of the usefulness of the concept of national character. I am not here defending the *term* "national character," which has the advantage of wide use and acceptance, and has also certain drawbacks. In my considered opinion the term "national character" has more practical advantages, and fewer important shortcomings than any other short title applicable to this subject. However, I do not quarrel with any one who uses some other name for this concept. See Appendix A.

2. The contrast here is of course particularly striking. England attained political unity, although under foreign rulers after 800. Since William the Conqueror no foreign ruler has gained control of the government by force. To go a little deeper, England may be said to have acquired cultural unity by the sixteenth century and political stability after 1688. The island of Great Britain has been one nation since 1707. As a "tight little island" it has developed unusual unity in national character in the best sense, in spite of great original diversities in language and culture between the wild Highlands and the lush and civilized southern counties.

Italian history on the other hand reverses the process. Culturally united and politically independent, although disunited, in the fourteenth and fifteenth centuries, she fell under Spanish and

French domination in the sixteenth, and remained under the Austrian Hapsburgs from the early eighteenth century until the middle of the nineteenth century. But Italian governments during this period were Italian, not alien, despite the fact that they depended in the ultimate case upon alien military power. At this time the political disunity of Italy was great enough to lend some force to the gibe that "Italy is only a geographical expression."

3. The RAND Corporation, with headquarters at Santa Monica, Calif., carries out large research projects in many fields of science and engineering, principally for the U.S. Air Force. From time to time it publishes unclassified articles on topics related to national defense, including those in the social sciences.

Notes to Section 11

1. Milton Eisenhower in his report to the President on Latin America (59) speaks of "genuine understanding on which fruitful co-operation must be based."

Notes to Section 12

1. National policy, strictly speaking, should be referred to as "national policies," as it properly varies in respect to different nations. Our foreign policy in respect to Poland, for example, is made up of many factors. Part is based upon our national character and aspirations. Evidently an equal part is based upon the Polish character and aspirations. Other influences are: Our allies, Poland's allies, and the history of Polish-American relations. As Nicolson says (24A), foreign policy must necessarily include a consideration of foreigners. At a given time special economic, political or military situations may have great influence on policy. All of this is set forth in such books as Marshall's *The Limits of Foreign Policy* (62A), Kennan's *Realities of American Foreign Policy* (62B) and Acheson's *Power and Diplomacy* (62C).

2. Bierce (as quoted by Lasswell and Kaplan, 27) defined revolution as "an abrupt change in the form of misgovernment."

3. Ortega y Gasset has said of Spain since the seventeenth century: "Beginning with the Monarchy and continuing with the Church, no national power in all that time has thought of anything outside itself. When did the heart—in the last analysis, a

foreign heart—of Spanish monarch or Spanish church ever beat for ends that were profoundly Spanish? Never." (64A, p. 39) As quoted by Deutsch.

4. This is similar to the statement that most conservatives are worshippers of some dead radical.

Notes to Section 13

1. Some historians place little credence on Stalin's explanation to Churchill of why he signed an agreement with Germany in 1939, as reported by Churchill and by Alanbrooke.

Stalin's biographer, Isaac Deutscher, in his *Stalin, a Political Biography*, pp. 426-445, analyses Stalin's motives as follows: Alarmed by his isolation at the time of the Munich crisis, he sought alliance with one side or the other, and seemed to prefer the Allies. His overtures were rudely rebuffed by Chamberlain, who dispatched a joint Franco-British military mission only after Russo-German talks had been initiated in July, 1939, and sent, at that, low-ranking officers, which Stalin took as an insult. Even after signing with Hitler he retained his respect for the French Army. At first he did not feel the Allies would go to war over Poland, but he changed his mind about that.

2. Compare the following: "Conrad when asked in 1914 [before England entered World War I] what England would do, felt confident in asserting that if England did come into the war then, no matter who might want to make peace at the end of six months at the cost of right and justice, England would keep on fighting for years and, if necessary, alone." Quoted by Ginsberg (16).

Notes to Appendix A

1. These goals are rather sharply oriented toward Western concepts and would not apply to many of the non-Western nations.

2. Deutsch uses communication here in his own technical sense to mean "the observable ability of certain groups of men and women to share with each other a wide range of whatever might be in their minds, and their observable inability to share these things nearly as widely with outsiders. We all know that men can share with each other much more easily what is in their hands than what is in their minds. . . ." Deutsch makes communication (in

this technical sense meaning the sharing of "information" in his technical sense) the central measurable criterion of the unity of groups of people.

Notes to Appendix B

1. Ginsberg says: "The relation is one of reciprocal inter-action rather than causality. (16, p. 136)" Actually in the relation described the same Operation B may act as the cause of Operation C, and may itself be the effect or result of Operation A. Then there may be a feedback from C to A. So causality is by no means ruled out of this network. Causality merely acts as a part of a complicated network, rather than as a simple straight-line sequence.

2. Elsewhere Lasswell and Kaplan (27, p. xix) deplore the confusion of thought and expression in political science. Their statements, which follow, would be equally applicable to many of the other social sciences and certainly to studies of national character. They say: "confusions, in political theory as elsewhere, have markedly interfered with fruitful research; certainly such confusions enter into the common disparagement of the political insights of the past and the widespread despair of what might be attained in this area in the future. But obscurity, vagueness, and ambiguity are *not* inherent in the subject matter of political science [or national character]; *they are inescapable only when no effort is made to escape them.*" (Square brackets and emphasis added.)

I fully concur. Much of the present lack of clearness in foreign intelligence production *is* escapable and is also inexcusable, now after two decades of experience.

BIBLIOGRAPHY

A book is not the end of a voyage
but the beginning.
—Holbrook Jackson.

The following references open the doors for the fruitful pursuit and further development of the many aspects of national character and its applications to foreign intelligence. These many aspects could be touched on only briefly in the text of an introductory study of the present kind.

I. Introduction

(1) McGarr, Major General L. C., "Education and National Security." *Military Review,* 40 (1960), July, 3-11.

(1A) Steiner, Zara S., *The State Department and the Foreign Service; The Wriston Report—Four Years Later.* Center of International Studies, Princeton, N. J., Princeton Univ. Press, 1958.

A sincere and vivid firsthand picture of conditions. Opinions may differ about the efficiency of our Department of State near the top level, but no one can overlook the neglects in the leadership and development of the rank and file for many years.

(2) Thayer, Charles W., *Diplomat.* New York, Harper, 1959.

Presents one part of the picture in a vivid and readable form.

(3) U. S. Senate, Foreign Relations Committee, *Study of U. S. Foreign Policy.*

Fifteen reports by different institutions. U. S. Senate, 1959 and 1960.

(4) Rockefeller Brothers Fund, *The Mid-Century Challenge to U. S. Foreign Policy,* Special Studies Project Report I. Garden City, N. Y., Doubleday, 1959.

(5) Sulzberger, C[yrus] L., *What's Wrong with U. S. Foreign Policy?* New York, Harcourt, Brace, 1959.

(6) Lederer, William J., and Eugene Burdick, *The Ugly American.* New York, Norton, 1958.

The tendency to attend to surface conditions and the failure to penetrate to the roots are all too true.

(7) Kertesz, Stephen D., and M. A. Fitzsimmons, Eds., *Diplomacy in a Changing World.* Notre Dame, Ind., Notre Dame Univ. Press, 1960.

(7A) Pettee, George S., *The Future of American Secret Intelligence.* Washington, D. C., Infantry Journal Press, 1946.

(7B)   Rusk, Dean, as quoted by Wallace Carroll, *New York Times,* March 17, 1961, p. 10, col. 3.

   The Secretary of State said, "It is the concern of the Department of State that the American people are safe and secure; defense is not a monopoly concern of the Department of Defense."

   This talk, which was said to have been sent out to every United States diplomatic and consular post, is an up-to-date confirmation of the position taken in the Preface and Introduction of this book in regard to the fundamental importance of the Department of State and of an understanding of foreign peoples, for our national security.

(8)   Platt, Washington, *Guidance from Uncertain Evidence —A Program for Progress in Intelligence and Foreign Relations.* In preparation.

   This will present an advanced study of the principles and methods which can lead to progress when operating in the great area of Uncertain Evidence.

(8A)   Abel, Theodore, "The Operation Called Verstehen," in Feigl, Herbert, and Max Brodbeck, Eds., *Readings in the Philosophy of Science.* New York, Appleton-Century-Crofts, 1953, p. 677.

(8B)   McGovern, William, *Strategic Intelligence and the Shape of Tomorrow.* Chicago, Regnery, 1961.

2. National Character—A Preliminary Statement

(9)   Morison, Elting E., Ed., *The American Style; Essays in Value and Performance. A Report of the Dedham Conference.* New York, Harper and Massachusetts Institute of Technology, Center for International Studies, 1958.

   This report includes the article by Rostow to which I have referred.

(9A)   Rostow, Walt W., *The United States in the World Arena; An Essay in Recent History.* New York, Harper, 1960.

(10) Lindzey, Gardner, Ed., *Assessment of Human Motives.* New York, Rinehart, 1958.

(11) Ginsberg, M., "National Character," *British Journal of Psychology*, 32 (1942), 183-205.

> This excellent summary refers to the "collective life of nations." Ginsberg says, "It is unwise to study persons acting individually, rather than as part of a group."

(12) Riesman, David, *et al.*, *The Lonely Crowd* (abridged) Garden City, New York, Doubleday (Anchor Books), 1953, p. 18.

> I concur with Orville Prescott, who, in the Feb. 1, 1960, *New York Times*, calls this "the most influential and important of all the books that view the current state of our society with considerable alarm—in spite of the sociological jargon in which it is written."

(13) Klineberg, Otto, *Tensions Affecting International Understanding—A Survey of Research.* New York, Social Science Research Council, Bulletin 62, 1950.

> A well-rounded survey which clearly indicates the present shortcoming of the purely "scientific" approach to national character. Many scientific writings in anthropology, psychology and psychiatry might well leave the reader with an exaggerated idea of the practical assistance which science can now offer toward understanding character.

(14) Stevenson, Adlai E., *Friends and Enemies: What I Learned in Russia.* New York, Harper, 1958.

(15) U. S. Advisory Commission on Information, *Fourteenth Annual Report.* Washington, D. C., U. S. Government Printing Office, 1958, pp. 42-43.

> Phil D. Reed, August, 1958, says: "Met halfway the [Russian] people are friendly and warm. They laugh easily and have a sense of humor much like our own. Until so met they are dead-pan."

(16) Ginsberg, Morris, *Reason and Unreason in Society; Essays in Sociology and Social Philosophy.* Cambridge, Mass., Harvard Univ. Press, 1948.

> He says much concisely and wisely.

3. Personal Character

(16A) Guilford, Joy P., *Personality*. New York, McGraw-Hill, 1959.

(17) Neider, Charles, *Autobiography of Mark Twain*. New York, Harper, 1959.

(18) Klineberg, Otto, *Social Psychology*, Revised Edition. New York, Holt, 1954. Readable, understandable, reliable.

(19) Rapoport, Anatol, *Operational Philosophy, Integrating Knowledge and Action*. New York, Harper, 1953.
A stimulating book which carries the reader much further than he has to go for our present purposes.

4. Scientific Aspects of Personal and Group Character

(20) Potter, David M., *People of Plenty; Economic Abundance and the American Character*. Chicago, Univ. of Chicago Press, 1954.
The first half of this book gives the best statement available of what I mean here by national character.

(21) Kluckhohn, Clyde, and H. A. Murray, Eds., *Personality in Nature, Society and Culture*, second edition. New York, Knopf, 1953.
A veritable encyclopedia on these subjects.

(21A) Medawar, Peter B., *The Uniqueness of the Individual*. New York, Basic Books, 1957.

(21B) ———, *The Future of Man*. London, Methuen, 1960.

(22) Adorno, Theodore W., *et al.*, *The Authoritarian Personality*. New York, Harper, 1950.

(23) Linton, Ralph, *Cultural Background of Personality*. New York, McGraw-Hill, 1959, p. 31.

(23A) Malinowski, Bronislaw, *A Scientific Theory of Culture*. Chapel Hill, N. C., Univ. of N. C. Press, 1944; N. Y., Oxford Univ. Press, 1960.

(23B) Shapiro, Harry L., *Aspects of Culture*. New Brunswick, N. J., Rutgers Univ. Press, 1957.

(24) Gorer, Geoffrey, "National Character; Theory and Practice," p. 57 in Mead, Margaret, and Rhoda Metraux, Eds., *The Study of Culture at a Distance*. Chicago, Univ. of Chicago Press, 1953.

5. Group Character—Practical Workings

(24A) Nicolson, Sir Harold, *National Character and National Policy*. Nottingham, University College, 1938.

(25) Sorokin, Pitirim A., *Society, Culture and Personality: Their Structure and Dynamics*. New York, Harper, 1947.

(26) Snyder, Richard C., and H. H. Wilson, Eds., *Roots of Political Behavior; Introduction to Government and Politics*. New York, American Book Co., 1949. The reference is to Chapter 5, "Society and Politics; Group Structure."

(27) Lasswell, Harold D., and A. Kaplan, *Power and Society; A Framework for Political Inquiry*. New Haven, Yale Univ. Press, 1950.

This covers in detail many points regarding the applications of group character which are specifically applicable to the present study.

(27A) Barker, Sir Ernest, *National Character and Factors in Its Formation*. London, Harper, 1957.

An excellent discussion of the meaning of national character, emphasizing the predominant character of the individuals within a nation, and giving only passing mention of the character of the nation when acting as such. In the formation of national character Barker considers: Material factors—genetic, geographic and economic. Then spiritual factors—political; religious; language, literature and thought; ideas and systems of education.

(28) Commager, Henry S., *The American Mind; Thought and Character Since the 1880's*. New Haven, Yale Univ. Press, 1950.

An interesting study of the individuality and character of a specific nation. A good example of a national character description.

(29) Lazarsfeld, Paul F., and W. Thielens, *The Academic Mind.* Glencoe, Ill., Free Press, 1958.

(29A) Kohn, Hans, *The Mind of Germany.* New York, Scribner, 1960.

(30) Snow, C[harles] P., *The Masters.* New York, Macmillan, 1951, p. 107.

(31) Fouillée, Alfred, *Esquisse psychologique des peuples européens.* Paris, F. Alcan, 1903.

(32) General Orders 201, GHQ, AEF, 1918.

A commendation of the First Division, AEF.

(33) Thomas, Hugh, Ed., *The Establishment.* London, A. Blond, 1959.

The writers fail to point out how much the existence of a group of men in Britain who know and understand each other, adds greatly to the strength and efficiency of the government, and to the top management of civil activities in the United Kingdom.

(33A) Middleton, Drew, "British Rule Tied to Upper Classes." *The New York Times,* Feb. 1, 1959, p. 8, col. 1.

(34) Riesman, David, *The Study of National Character: Some Observations on the American Case,* Harvard Library Bulletin, 13 (1959), p. 13.

An excellent summary of the present status of some of our best ideas on national character. Some of this is in accordance with the views expressed in the present book and some is not.

(35) Key, Valdimer O., *Politics, Parties and Pressure Groups,* Fourth Edition, New York, Crowell, 1958.

This goes deeply into the mechanics of government.

(36) Lasswell, Harold D., Daniel Lerner, and C. E. Rothwell, *The Comparative Study of Elites; An Introduction and Bibliography.* Stanford, Calif., Stanford Univ. Press, 1952.

Contains an excellent bibliography.

(37)   Conway, [William] Martin, *The Crowd in Peace and War*. New York, Longmans, Green, 1915.

(38)   Platt, Washington, *Strategic Intelligence Production— Basic Principles*. New York, Praeger, 1957.

This is intended as a basic contribution to the knowledge, training and point of view which will assist the intelligence officer to draw the soundest conclusions from the available data, and to express these in the form most helpful to the ultimate users of strategic intelligence.

(38A) Cantril, Hadley, *Soviet Leaders and Mastery Over Man*. New Brunswick, N. J., Rutgers Univ. Press, 1960.

(38B) Holt, Robert T., and R. W. van de Welde, *Strategic Psychological Operations and American Foreign Policy*. Chicago, Univ. of Chicago Press, 1960.

Presents the concept of the "crucial audience," an aggregate of people which, if converted to the United States point of view, could have an important favorable influence on the action of the foreign nation in the given situation. If hostile, their influence could be important against us.

(38C) Shirer, William L., *Rise and Fall of the Third Reich; A History of Nazi Germany*. New York, Simon and Schuster, 1960.

An outstanding study of national character and an excellent example of the effect of *compulsion* upon civilized human beings. Contains sidelights on other points made in the present volume.

6. Basic Beliefs or Fundamental Philosophy

(39)   Ortega y Gassett, José, *Concord and Liberty*. New York, Norton, 1946.

Some aspects of fundamental philosophy are presented with unusual simplicity and clearness.

(40)   Kluckhohn, Clyde, quoted by Northrop in reference (45).

(41)   Benedict, Ruth, *The Chrysanthemum and the Sword; Patterns of Japanese Culture.* Boston, Houghton Mifflin, 1946.

(41A) Douglas, Justice William O., *A Living Bill of Rights.* New York, Doubleday, 1961.

(42)   Northrop, F[ilmer] S. C., *The Meeting of East and West; An Inquiry concerning World Understanding.* New York, Macmillan, 1946.

(43)   ———, Ed., *Ideological Differences and World Order; Studies in the Philosophy of Science of the World's Cultures.* New Haven, Conn., Yale Univ. Press, 1949.

(43A) ———, *Philosophical Anthropology and Practical Politics—A Prelude to War or to Just Law.* New York, Macmillan, 1960.

        (42) and (43A) are vigorous statements of fundamental philosophy requiring some philosophical background for full understanding. (42) contains enlightening specific examples of national character.

(44)   Morris, Charles W., *Paths of Life; Preface to a World Religion.* New York, Harper, 1942.

(44A) Bozeman, Adda B., *Politics and Culture in International History.* Princeton, N. J., Princeton Univ. Press, 1960.

        Long in time (several millenniums) and broad in coverage (global), this book provides an excellent background for any study of international relations. Touching on the subject which I have here called Fundamental Philosophy or Basic Beliefs, Bozeman points out that "each of the regions of the earth . . . has its own traditions of life and thought which antedate, in many cases by millenniums, both the conception of the one world and that of two." He goes on to say that these fundamental philosophies in Asia, Africa and elsewhere were often temporarily submerged by the impact of Western thought. These deep Basic Beliefs are now emerging again. The discussion in the

Introduction throws much light on these beliefs as they affect current problems of international relations. This discussion is the best that I have seen in its practical applications—hence in its pertinence to this aspect of national character. Pertinent also are Bozeman's remarks (pp. 466-467) about Venetian character and its practical effects.

(45) Northrop, F[ilmer] S. C., *The Importance of Deductively Formulated Theory in Ethics and Social and Legal Theory*, from *Structure, Method and Meaning. Essays in Honor of Henry M. Sheffer.* New York, Liberal Arts Press, 1951, p. 10.

7. National Character—The Character of a Nation

(45A) De Gaulle, Charles, *Salvation, 1944-1946; The Memoirs of Charles De Gaulle*, Translated by Richard Howard. New York, Simon and Schuster, 1960.

(46) Deutsch, Karl W., *Nationalism and Social Communication; An Inquiry into the Foundations of Nationality.* Cambridge, Mass., and New York, Technology Press of MIT and Wiley, 1953.

Excellent. Discusses character-forming agencies. Contains much that is essential to the thesis of the present book. Presented in an original and stimulating form.

(47) Beard, Charles A., *The Economic Basis of Politics.* New York, Knopf, 1934, p. 67, as quoted by Lasswell and Kaplan (27), p. 32.

(47A) Reshetar, John S., *Problems of Analyzing and Predicting Soviet Behavior.* Garden City, N. Y., Doubleday, 1955.

An interesting study of the problems of estimating the behavior of a foreign country. In my opinion our present opportunities for making such estimates are better than this study would lead us to believe.

(48) Burns, James M., and J. W. Petalson, *Government by*

the People; the Dynamics of American National Government, Third edition. New York, Prentice-Hall, 1957.

(48A) Brogan, Denis W., *France.* Chicago, Life Book Department, 1961.

Pertinent to the discussion of the two-party system in this section is Brogan's statement: "For France to have a two-party system, France would have to have had a different history."

(49) Mack Smith, Denis M, *Italy: A Modern History.* Ann Arbor, Mich., Univ. of Michigan Press, 1959.

(50) Nelson, Lowry, Jr., *Yale Review,* Winter, 1960.
A review of the above.

(50A) Akram, Lt. Col. A. I., "On Relative Strengths," *Pakistan Army Journal,* Vol. 1, No. 4, 1958. Digested in *Military Review, 39,* July, 1959.

(50B) Knorr, Klaus E., *War Potential of Nations.* Princeton, N. J., Princeton Univ. Press, 1956, Chapters on "The Will to Fight."

(51) Spalding, H. N., *Civilization in East and West. An Introduction to the Study of Human Progress.* London, Oxford Univ. Press, 1939, p. 123.

(51A) Lindzey, Gardner, Ed., *Handbook of Social Psychology.* Cambridge, Mass., Addison-Wesley, 1954. Chapter 26, *The Study of Modal Personality and Socio Cultural Systems,* by Inkeles, Alex., and D. J. Levinson.

(51B) Hoffer, Eric, *The True Believer; Thoughts on the Nature of Mass Movements.* New York, Harper, 1951.

Prescott as cited at Ref. (12) describes this as: "aphoristic, realistic, somewhat cynical reflections on the nature of mass movements and the nature of the men who join them. One of the most intellectually exciting and disturbing books of our time."

8. The Spirit of Youth and Its Opposite

(51C) Fleming, Peter, *The Sixth Column.* London, Hart-Davis, 1951.

9. Sources of Information on the Characters of Specific Nations

(52)   Lerner, Max, *America as a Civilization*. New York, Simon and Schuster, 1957.

(53)   Middleton, Drew, *These Are the British*. New York, Knopf, 1957.

(53A) Human Relations Area Files, New Haven, Conn.

       The coverage of different countries is very uneven in extent and in quality. In some cases national character receives consideration. Details of this important collection are given at the end of the Supplement hereto.

(53B) Mead, Margaret, Ed., *Cultural Patterns and Technical Change*. New York, New American Library (Mentor Books), 1955.

       A reprint of the original edition published by UNESCO.

(53C) Santayana, George, "The Best in English Character," from *Soliloquies in England and Later Soliloquies*. New York, Scribner, 1922.

(53D) Barker, Sir Ernest, Ed., *The Character of England*. London, Oxford Univ. Press, 1947.

See also publications on the characters of specific nations given as a Supplement at the end of this Bibliography.

10. Difficulties in Using National Character as an Intelligence Tool

(54)   [Beaconsfield, Lord] Benjamin Disraeli, *Sybil or The Two Nations*. London, Henry Colburn, 1845.

(55)   Joseph, Franz M., Ed., *As Others See Us; The United States Through Foreign Eyes*. Princeton, N. J., Princeton Univ. Press, 1959.

(56)   Schlesinger, Arthur W., Jr. *New York Times Book Review*, Dec. 20, 1959.

       A review of the above book.

(57) Toynbee, Arnold J., *A Study of History* (10 vol.), as abridged by D. C. Somervell in 2 vols. London, Oxford Univ. Press, 1957.

11. Levels of Investigation Leading to Top Achievement

(58) Steiner, Zara S., *The State Department and the Foreign Service; The Wriston Report Four Years Later.* See (1A).

To get a picture of the present situation one does not have to go further than this report and the references therein.

(59) *New York Times,* January 4, 1959.

(60) Snow, C[harles] P., *Strangers and Brothers,* London, Macmillan, 1951, p. 308.

12. Critical Review of Tentative Conclusions

(61) Conant, James B., *On Understanding Science.* New Haven, Conn., Yale Univ. Press, 1947.

(62) Neill, Humphrey B., *The Art of Contrary Thinking.* Caldwell, Idaho, Caxton, 1956.

(62A) Marshall, Charles B., *The Limits of Foreign Policy.* New York, Holt, 1954.

(62B) Kennan, George F., *Realities of American Foreign Policy.* Princeton, N. J., Princeton Univ. Press, 1954.

(62C) Acheson, Dean, *Power and Diplomacy.* Cambridge, Mass., Harvard Univ. Press, 1958.

13. Examples of the Unique Role of National Character in Intelligence

(63) Storrs, Sir Ronald, *Orientations.* London, Nicholson and Watson, 1937.

(64) Taylor, Alan J. P., *The Trouble Makers; Dissent over Foreign Policy, 1792-1939.* Bloomington, Ind., Indiana Univ. Press, 1958.

(64A) Ortega y Gassett, José, *Invertebrate Spain.* New York, Norton, 1937.

(65)   Bryant, Arthur, *The Turn of the Tide; A History of the War Years Based on the Diaries of Field-Marshal Lord Alanbrooke, Chief of the Imperial General Staff.* Garden City, N. Y., Doubleday, 1957, pp. 381-3.

(66)   Churchill, Winston S., *Second World War; The Gathering Storm.* Boston, Houghton Mifflin and Cooperation Publ. Co., 1948-1953, p. 391.

(67)   Ludwig, Emil, "The German Mind," *Atlantic Monthly*, Feb., 1938.

(68)   Fleming, Peter, *Operation Sea Lion.* New York, Simon and Schuster, 1957.

(69)   Wheatley, Ronald, *Operation Sea Lion; German Plans for the Invasion of England, 1939-1942.* New York, Oxford Univ. Press, 1958, especially pp. 4, 5, 16, 82, 85.

(70)   Churchill, Winston S., *A History of the English-Speaking Peoples; The Great Democracies*, Vol. 4. New York, Dodd, Mead, 1958, as quoted in an excellent review by Sir Harold Nicolson, *New York Times Book Review*, March 16, 1958.

Appendices

(71)   Herz, Frederick, *Nationality in History and Politics.* New York, Oxford Univ. Press, 1944, pp. 13-24.

(72)   Carr, Edward H., *Nationalism and After.* New York, Macmillan, 1945.

(73)   Brinton, [Clarence] Crane, *Ideas and Men: The Story of Western Thought.* New York, Prentice-Hall, 1950, pp. 500-502.
         This whole book evidently contains much that will add to the knowledge and understanding of anyone interested in foreign intelligence and the individuality of different foreign peoples.

(74)   [Beaconsfield, Lord] Benjamin Disraeli, *The Spirit of Whiggism, 1836*, cited by Deutsch (46, p. 7).

(75)   Schuerch, Ernst, *Sprachpolitische Erinnerungen.* Bern, Paul Haupt Verlag, 1943, pp. 36-37.

(76) Mills, Charles W., *The Power Elite*. New York, Oxford Univ. Press, 1956.

(77) Trevelyan, George M., *Clio, A Muse, and Other Essays*. London, Longmans, Green, 1913.
      The title essay first published in 1904.

(78) Klineberg, Otto, "A Science of National Character," *Journal of Social Psychology* 19 (1944), pp. 147-62.

(79) Eysenck, Hans J., *Sense and Nonsense in Psychology*. Baltimore, Penguin Books, Revised, 1958.
      Especially chapters on "Can Personality Be Measured?" and "Politics and Personality."

The High Spots

We see from the above that the subject of national character in foreign intelligence applies principles and methods derived from the social, behavioral and natural sciences, as well as from history, philosophy, and the principles of foreign intelligence.

However, the more important disciplines and concepts considered in the present study are those listed and italicized immediately below. These are followed in each case by some of the key references thereto. This high-spotting may save the reader's time in making his initial exploration of this field.

Numbers in parentheses indicate the references given in the Bibliography.

Social Psychology. Klineberg (18) provides the layman with one of the best introductions to this subject. He gives a scholarly but understandable statement of the basic principles without jargon.

Political Science. All of us know the elements of government. Lasswell and Kaplan (27) give a brilliant, but somewhat abstract, discussion of definitions and principles. They make *political power* the unifying theme. Their book is so stimulating that it is well worth the effort to read it.

Nationality. This is an important concept in political science and fundamental in any consideration of national character. Deutsch (46) has written the study most pertinent to the present book. He uses "communication" (in his own technical sense) as the basic consideration. Any one reading this book will gain much understanding that is pertinent to our present purpose.

Personality and Character. If one is willing to plunge into the technical jargon of psychology, psychiatry and other *psy's,* he will find much of value in *Personality in Nature, Society and Culture* (21) by Kluckhohn, Murray and Schneider. He will also find much that has as yet no useful application to our present problems.

Fundamental Philosophy. See Northrop (42 and 43). He is the outstanding writer. An elementary introduction to this point of view is provided by Morris (44).

National Character. By all means start with the general statement given by Potter (20), pages 1-72. Then Ginsberg (11 and 16), then Riesman's *The Lonely Crowd* (12) in that order. For examples describing the national character of specific nations see the Supplement to this Bibliography.

Foreign Relations and Diplomacy. There are plenty of good books by experts on past and current situations. See, for example, (2), (62A), (62B), (62C).

Shortcomings of Modern U. S. Foreign Policy. The Diplomat by Thayer (2), *The Ugly American* (6) and Steiner (1A), preferably in that order. These are not exaggerated. Then further reading should follow.

Foreign Intelligence, also called strategic intelligence. See Kent on *Strategic Intelligence,* Princeton, 1949. I have also the temerity to suggest my own book on *Strategic Intelligence Production—Basic Principles* (38). This is an elementary statement of some of the principles at the very *foundation* of producing good intelligence. It also points out some current remediable shortcomings in our methods.

The Broad View of Human History. Worthwhile broad views of human history and thought are given with originality and insight by Brinton (73) and Hoffer (50B). A broadening and thought-provoking book, not cited in the present bibliography, is: Muller, H. J., *The Uses of the Past: Profiles of Former Societies,* New York, Oxford Univ. Press, 1952.

SUPPLEMENT TO
BIBLIOGRAPHY

Publications on the Characters of Specific Nations as Discussed in Section 9

When a publication in this Supplement is also listed in the main part of the Bibliography, its reference number there is shown in parenthesis.

The United States

Riesman, David, *Cultural and Social Factors in National Strength: The United States.* Washington, D. C., Industrial College of the Armed Forces, Publication L59-62, 1958-59.

Commager, Henry S., *America in Perspective; The United States through Foreign Eyes.* New York, Random House, 1947.

———, *The American Mind, Thought and Character Since the 1880's* (28).

Lerner, Max, *America as a Civilization*, (52).

Brogan, Denis W., *The American Character.* New York, Knopf, revised ed., 1957.

———, *America in the Modern World.* New Brunswick, N. J., Rutgers Univ. Press, 1960.

221

Barghoorn, Frederick C., *Soviet Image of the United States; Study in Distortion*. Harcourt, Brace, 1950.

Baldwin, Leland D., *Meaning of America; Essays Toward an Understanding of the American Spirit*. Pittsburgh, Pa., Univ. of Pittsburgh Press, 1955. Northrop, F. S. C. (42) for Fundamental Philosophy.

Siegfried, André, *Nations Have Souls*, listed here under France.

Latin America

Mexico

Lewis, Oscar, *Life in a Mexican Village; Tepozlan Restudied*. Urbana, Ill., Univ. of Illinois Press, 1951.

In this well-rounded village study an American anthropologist depicts with some psychological sophistication the ethos or character of Mexican villagers. He includes materials showing how the natives categorize one another.

Martin, Sylvia (Pass), *You Meet Them in Mexico*. New Brunswick, N. J., Rutgers Univ. Press, 1948.

Has many concrete examples of Mexican behavior and attitudes.

Northrop, F. S. C. (42) for Fundamental Philosophy.

Brazil

Tavares de Sá Hernane, *The Brazilians; People of Tomorrow*. New York, John Day Co., 1947.

This book, written by a Brazilian intellectual, is rather general in its approach. Chapters II, III and IV, as well as the last three chapters, are of especial interest. Brazilian-American relations are treated. The entire book gives a picture of Brazilian character from a Brazilian point of view, combined with much information on politics and history.

Uruguay

Fitzgibbon, Russell H., *Uruguay; Portrait of Democracy*. New Brunswick, N. J., Rutgers Univ. Press, 1954.

England and Scotland

Santayana, George, "The Best in British Character," from *Soliloquies in England and Later Soliloquies* (53C).

Middleton, Drew, *These are the British* (53).

————, Article in *The New York Times*, February 1, 1957, on *The Establishment* (33A).

Certainly an eye-opener. See also (33B).

Pont's *The British Character* (from *Punch*). London, Fontana Books, 1956 (first published 1938).

Northrop, F[ilmer] S. C., (42) for Fundamental Philosophy.

Barker, Sir Ernest, Ed., (53D)

In *National Character and the Factors in Its Formation* (27A), Barker gives a delightful discussion of the formation of English character from the historical and institutional points of view. He considers this subject under each of seven important factors.

McLaren, Moray, *The Scots*. Harmondsworth, Middlesex, Penguin Books, 1951.

Gorer, Geoffrey, *Exploring English Character*. New York, Criterion Books, 1955.

An interesting exploration of the character of English men and women as far as this can be accomplished by questionnaire. There is no consideration of the character of England or the United Kingdom as a nation when acting as such.

Western Europe

Germany

Valentin, Veit, *The German People, Their History and Civilization from the Holy Roman Empire to the Third Reich*. New York, Knopf, 1946.

Lowie, Robert H., *Toward Understanding Germany*. Chicago, Univ. of Chicago Press, 1954.

This book is by an American anthropologist who was born in Vienna. Using an ethnographic approach and gaining considerable depth in recent history, the author achieves a rare sense of detachment in describing the German character and some of its variants.

Northrop, F[ilmer] S. C., (42) for Fundamental Philosophy.

France

Schoenbrun, David, *As France Goes*. New York, Harper, 1957.
> See especially chapter on "Manners, Morals and Mores of the French" and the final chapter.

Wylie, Laurence, *Village in the Vaucluse*. Cambridge, Mass., Harvard Univ. Press, 1958.

Siegfried, André, *Nations Have Souls*. New York, Putnam, 1952.
> This work by a Frenchman analyzes in a somewhat literary manner French, English, German, Russian, and American national characters. Although far from rigorous social science, this is a good if highly impressionistic study.

Cooper, Duff [Lord Norwich], *Talleyrand*. London, Jonathan Cape, 1932.
> Cooper quotes (page 263) a British estimate of French national character. In 1815 Lord Castlereagh wrote to the head of the British mission in Paris: "I agree with you that Talleyrand cannot be relied on, and yet I know not on whom His Majesty can better depend. . . . The fact is that France is a den of thieves and brigands, and they can only be governed by criminals like themselves."
>
> By contrast, as a very up-to-date reference, the reader should read the whole of the little book by Brogan (48A) for a brief and excellent summary.

Italy

Banfield, Edward C., *The Moral Basis of a Backward Society*. Glencoe, Ill., Free Press, 1958.
> This study by an American deals primarily with the very "family-oriented" southern Italian peasant, his attitudes toward his community and the state. The relation of ethos to voting behavior is treated. There is more

moralistic bias on the part of the author than would seem desirable for objectivity, and the book should be read with this in mind.

Sforza, Carlo, *The Real Italians; Study in European Psychology*. New York, Columbia Univ. Press, 1942.

A broad coverage with special interest in national character and political life.

Spain

Pitt-Rivers, Julian A., *People of the Sierras*. New York, Criterion Books, 1954.

This Andalusian community study is, while sociological in approach, concerned with the values and attitudes of villagers. Because of interest in social groups, attitudes discussed are often class-stratified.

Siegfried, André, *Nations Have Souls*. Listed here under France.

Norway

Rodnick, David, *The Norwegians; A Study in National Culture*. Washington, D. C., Public Affairs Press, 1955.

Stresses national character with individual treatment of different socio-economic groups. It is written from the viewpoint of an American social scientist, and uses some psychological terminology, but on a low level of sophistication.

Finland

Hall, Wendy, *Green Gold and Granite*. London, Max Parrish, 1953.

Not social-scientific. The Finnish national character is sketched subjectively in common-sense terms. The treatment is neither systematic nor complete. See Chapter IV on "The Finnish Character," also Chapter XVIII.

For Various Western European Nations

White, Theodore H., *Fire in the Ashes; Europe in Mid-Century*. New York, Sloane, 1953.

Vivid contrasting pictures of certain European nations in the early 1950's. The differences in national character are implicit. Reporting the results of a French study into the causes of American industrial superiority, White says (p. 366): "There was no particular little secret which was the clue to the big secret. The main clue was there for everyone to see and every visitor reported it—Americans just worked differently; there was an indefinable *spirit* that made Americans work harder, more efficiently, better, more together. *It was the spirit that was the clue.*" (The emphasis added is mine.)

U.S.S.R.

Russia

Bauer, Raymond A., Alex Inkeles, and Clyde Kluckhohn, *How the Soviet System Works*. Cambridge, Mass., Harvard Univ. Press, 1956.

This highly-recommended book covers the Soviet system from many viewpoints, with continual reference to national character and the character of specific groups. In addition, there is a chapter devoted to national character. The analysis is based upon interviews with refugees.

Dicks, Henry V., "Observations on Contemporary Russian Behavior," *Human Relations,* Vol. V, No. 2, 1952.

A long journal article, very tentative, based on some early refugee interviews. The underlying assumptions are Freudian, and a good part of the discussion is couched in somewhat clinical terms. However, a good common-sense picture of the Russian character emerges, especially with regard to authority and the individual.

Werth, Alexander, *The Year of Stalingrad*. London, Hamish Hamilton, 1946.

The main aspect of Russian character covered in depth here is the arousal of the Russian people through an appeal to nationalism during the Second World War.

Crankshaw, Edward, *Russia and the Russians*. New York, Viking Press, 1948.

The author is a historian and a journalist. During part of World War II he served with the British Military Mission to Moscow, and has had the opportunity for travel in Russia. The book is a sincere study—impressionistic, journalistic and imaginative. It shows a sympathetic insight into some aspects of life in European Russia.

One feels, however, the need of a broader basis for final judgment in the form of the impressions of others, also based on firsthand experience.

Barghoorn, Frederick C., *Soviet Russian Nationalism*. New York, Oxford Univ. Press, 1956.

Prof. Barghoorn is well-acquainted with the Russian language and people. The subject of this book is not Russian national character, but in discussing the growth of nationalism he necessarily describes and contrasts the reactions of the people in Russia proper with those of the Ukraine, Georgia and some other parts of the U.S.S.R. As the book is written from a real depth of understanding it has an unusual degree of reliability. It throws light on many aspects of the character of the peoples of U.S.S.R. as incidental to its main purpose.

Northrop, F. S. C. (Ref. 42) for Fundamental Philosophy.

Siegfried, André, Nations Have Souls. Listed here under France.

Smith, General Walter Bedell, *My Three Years in Moscow*. Philadelphia, Lippincott, 1950.

Throws light on the character of the Soviet "Power Elite" at that time which has many traits in common with the present time.

Custine, Astolphe, Marquis de, *Journey for Our Time; The*

Journals of the Marquis de Custine. Edited and translated by Phyllis P. Kohler, Introduction by Walter Bedell Smith. New York, Pellegrini and Cudahy, 1951.

The journeys were taken in the early 1840's. The number of traits of character which the Russians of those Czarist days had in common with the Russians of today is extraordinary. Amusing and illuminating as a study of national character.

Eastern Europe

Poland

Benet, Sula, "Patterns of Thought and Behavior in the Culture of Poland," in Margaret Mead and Rhoda Metraux, Eds., *The Study of Culture at a Distance.* Chicago, Univ. of Chicago Press, 1953.

A member of a large research project on contemporary national character gives a slightly romantic picture of the Polish attitudes toward war and defeat, with some historical background.

Super, Paul, *The Polish Tradition: an Interpretation of a Nation.* London, Allen and Unwin, 1939.

This book gives a broad outline of Polish national character, with considerable historical depth. Commonsense psychological terms are used. Especially useful is a chapter on the views of other nations, as seen by Poles.

Zawacki, Edmund, "The Polish National Spirit," in Bernadotte Schmitt, Editor, *Poland.* Berkeley and Los Angeles, Calif., Univ. of California Press, 1945, pp. 328-343.

An article written by an American during World War II. A somewhat laudatory sketch of Poland, emphasizing historical patriotism, love of freedom, religious toleration, and Christian political outlook.

Hungary

Trocsanyi, George, "The Hungarian National Character," in *The Hungarian Quarterly,* Volume 5, Number 1, Summer, 1939, pp. 195-204.

In this article a Hungarian sociologist attempts to describe an indigenous "core" character which might be regarded as the traditional character. This seems to be a solid sketch, with especial attention given to political attitudes.

Yugoslavia

Halpern, Joel, *Social and Cultural Change in a Serbian Village*, (Pre-Publication Monograph). Human Relations Area Files, New Haven, 1956.

This excellent and objective village study deals with the character of the Serbian villager throughout, but the chapter on ethos treats specifically with village attitudes, especially toward social change. Halpern cautions with regard to generalizing from the village to much larger units.

This work is also available under the title *A Serbian Village* (New York, Columbia Univ. Press, 1958). However, the chapter on ethos is not included.

Rumania

Benedict, Ruth, "History As It Appears to the Rumanians," which appears as a section with this title in Margaret Mead and Rhoda Metraux, Eds., *The Study of Culture at a Distance*. Chicago, Univ. of Chicago Press, 1953.

This article is interpretive, yet fairly conservative, using historical documentation. It points out the differences between the way Rumanians view their nation in history and the way the more nearly objective historian does, especially with regard to international power politics. Of limited use.

Benedict, Ruth, *Rumanian Culture and Behavior*. Mimeographed; distributed by Institute for Intercultural Studies, 15 West 77th St., New York 24, New York, 1943.

This is the complete study from which "History As It Appears to the Rumanians" was taken. It deals with modal behavior on the village level, and on the town and city level. Adult and child behavior are treated separately. A broad coverage is achieved, with many examples given.

Bulgaria

Sanders, Irwin T., *Balkan Village*, Lexington, Ky., Univ. of Kentucky Press, 1949.

A well-rounded village study by a sociologist, drawn from prewar and postwar field research. Considerable emphasis is put upon the political change after World War II. The village studied is representative of one region of Bulgaria, as well as having implications for the study of the Balkan peasant in general.

Greece

Mead, Margaret, *Cultural Patterns and Technical Change* (53B).

Nicolson, Sir Harold, *National Character and National Policy* (24A).

In this 13-page lecture Nicolson's brief, cogent summary of Greek character is unusually valuable.

Asia

Burma

Pye, Lucian W., *The Spirit of Burmese Politics.* Cambridge, Mass., Center for International Studies, Massachusetts Institute of Technology, 1959.

A preliminary report about Burmese character and its implications for Burmese politics. This little book is an exploratory work, based upon field work in Burma, which attempts to distill some hypotheses about national character and politics. It is to be followed by a more thorough study which should be excellent.

India

Murphy, Gardner, *In the Minds of Men.* New York, Basic Books, 1953.

A rather solid picture of Indian national character emerges from this book, which attacks very directly the problems of India's growth and America's relation to these problems. This book is a product of the UNESCO Tensions Project.

Steed, Gitel P., "Notes on an Approach to a Study of Personality Formation in a Hindu Village in Gujarat," in McKim Marriott (Ed.), *Village India*. Chicago, American Anthropological Association, Univ. of Chicago Press, 1955.

This long article combines a general discussion of implications of sociological and political factors on personality with a depth study of one individual in a Hindu village. The author's position on the concept of national or modal character is made explicit.

Northrop, F[ilmer] S. C., (42) for Fundamental Philosophy.

Gorer, Geoffrey, *Himalayan Village*. London, Michael Joseph, 1938.

This account of a primitive Indian mountain people is packed with character description. However, the uniqueness of the Lepchas described limits its usefulness for wider generalization.

Pakistan

Honigman, John J., and Richard N. Carrera, "Some Themes in Pakistan National Culture." Chapel Hill, N. C., Institute for Research in Social Science, Univ. of North Carolina, 1957. (Mimeographed)

This study, while limited, does attempt an analysis of popular communications media, chiefly of native writers' opinions, explicit and implicit, on Pakistani character in general. The analysis is not thorough enough to present a systematic picture.

Qureshi, Ishtiaq, *The Pakistani Way of Life*. London, William Heinemann, 1956.

A short book on the Pakistanis which describes, but does not analyze in any depth, many general national characteristics. This is to be found in the context of a rather general discussion of this new nation.

China

Snow, Edgar, *Red Star Over China*. New York, Random House, 1941.

This work, although generally marginal to the study of national character, contains an autobiography of Mao Tse-tung recorded by the authors, which affords much insight into the early development of the communist movement in China.

Smith, Arthur H., *Chinese Characteristics*. New York, Revell, 1894.

A remarkably complete survey of the Chinese character written with insight by a late nineteenth century missionary.

Lin, Yutang, *My Country and My People*. New York, Reynal and Hitchcock, 1935.

An excellent study. Chinese character is treated systematically and in detail.

Philippines

Batacan, Delfin F., *Looking at Ourselves; a Study of Our Peculiar Social Traits as People*. Manila, Philaw, 1956.

This very useful book gives several viewpoints (including those in the appendices) on Philippine national character. All use common-sense psychology. The book itself is devoted to an exhaustive discussion of Philippine character, and foreign opinions are discussed. The author himself is strongly oriented toward criticism, evidently in reaction against complacency, but the general tone of the discussion is scholarly, and the author seems aware of his limitations.

Indonesia

van Wulfften Palthe, P. M., *Psychological Aspects of the Indonesian Problem*. Leiden, The Netherlands, E. J. Brill, 1949.

This is a short book. The psychology seems amateurish, but it does give a Dutch viewpoint on native political psychology.

Thailand

Landon, K. P., *Siam in Transition*. Chicago, Univ. of Chicago Press, 1939.

A short chapter on Thai character and several chapters on Thai religion give a limited picture of Thai personality in general. This book was written by a professor of philosophy.

Blanchard, Wendell, *et al.*, *Thailand: Its People, Its Society, Its Culture*. New Haven, Conn., Human Relations Area Files, 1958.

A useful discussion of character and attitudes is included in this general survey. The degree of homogeneity of Thai national character is discussed. This book has a particularly exhaustive bibliography.

Laos

See *Area Handbook on Laos* in the Human Relations Area Files described at the end of this Supplement.

Japan

Zacharias, Ellis M., *Secret Missions; Story of an Intelligence Officer*. New York, Putnam, 1946.

Note especially the section on Japanese character beginning on page 62. This book is, however, inadequate as a study of national character. It shows the use of this factor in intelligence and propaganda activities with regard to Japan before and during World War II. Benedict, Ruth, *Chrysanthemum and the Sword* (41).

Middle Eastern Area

General

Lerner, Daniel, *The Passing of Traditional Society*. Glencoe, Ill., Free Press, 1958.

This unique book sums up a great deal of sociological research, much of which was done through questionnaires. Of especial interest is the analysis of how mass communications media facilitate the changing of certain attitudes as modernization occurs. Although the specific hypothesis being tested may not be of direct relevance, the discussion of character for Turkey, Lebanon, Egypt, Syria, Jordan and Iran is valuable.

Smith, Wilfred Cantwell, *Islam in Recent History*. Princeton, N. J., Princeton Univ. Press, 1957.

Discusses the character of the Islamic religion in general, but in addition the author also discusses its relation to various groups, including Christian Arabs, Muslim Arabs, Turks, Pakistanis, and Indians. Reactions to contact with Western Powers are also discussed, with insight, and the analysis goes considerably beyond the topic of religion alone.

Coon, Carleton, *Caravan*. New York, Holt, 1951.

This is one of the best general background works on the Middle East. It discusses some characteristics of various minorities, as well as the rather unique status of minority groups in this area.

Atiyah, Edward, *The Arabs*. Baltimore, Penguin Books, 1955.

Throws light on some aspects of Arab national character. See especially pages 46, 96, 233.

Fisher, Sydney N., Ed., *Social Forces in the Middle East*. Ithaca, N. Y., Cornell Univ. Press, 1955.

Although this book does not deal specifically with national character, it is of general interest, and deals separately with various groups and their problems of social adjustment. There is a well-organized bibliography which might be of use in research on specific problems.

Lewis, Bernard, *The Arabs in History*. London, Anchor Press, 1950.

An excellent historical treatise which gives (in Chapter VIII) a short but piercing analysis of Islamic society, conducted at a fairly high level of philosophical abstraction.

Nuseibeh, Hazem Z., *The Ideas of Arab Nationalism*. Ithaca, N. Y., Cornell Univ. Press, 1956.

Although biased, this book gives an interesting view of Arab nationalism from a non-Western standpoint. Because the book is general and historical, there is little treatment of characteristics from any psychological standpoint, but a general impression is presented.

Iran

Upton, Joseph M., *The History of Modern Iran*. Cambridge, Mass., Harvard Univ. Press, 1960.

An excellent social history of modern Iran. There is no systematic treatment of national character, but a general impression does emerge.

Gastil, Raymond D., *Iranian General Beliefs as Found in Middle Class Shiraz*. Ph.D. Thesis, Cambridge, Mass., Harvard University, 1958.

In spite of the fact that this work involves some very technical theoretical schemes, it might be of considerable use. It deals with the modal character of a specific group in Iran, approached from several points of view. Religious factors and the relation of the individual to society are given extensive treatment. This study included nearly a year's work in the field, utilizing the questionnaire method.

Iraq

Longrigg, Stephen H., and Frank Stokes, *Iraq*. London, Ernest Benn, 1958.

A short, superficial delineation of the character of various Iraqui groups is given. There is also a chapter on politics.

Israel

Spiro, Melford E., *Kibbutz; Venture in Utopia*. Cambridge, Mass., Harvard Univ. Press, 1956.

While primarily a case study of an ultra-cooperative group, this book deals throughout with the character of the *kibbutz* workers, who comprise an important minority in Israel.

Egypt

Wynn, Wilton, *Nasser of Egypt; The Search for Dignity.* Cambridge, Mass., Arlington Books, 1959.

This sympathetic book by a journalist describes the political career of Nasser. While there is little description of the national character of the Egyptian masses, Nasser, their leader, is well-depicted. The value of this study lies in its sympathetic treatment of Egyptian aspirations.

Human Relations Area Files

The Human Relations Area Files (HRAF) and the Area Handbooks published by the same nonprofit organization are a possible source of information on research on national character. The files themselves are maintained at the following universities:

University of Chicago
University of Colorado
Cornell University
Harvard University
University of Hawaii
Indiana University
State University of Iowa
University of Michigan
University of North Carolina
University of Oklahoma
University of Pennsylvania
University of Southern California
University of Utah
University of Washington
University of Southern Illinois
Yale University

Each member university has a set of the files. This includes photostatted pages from various books, monographs, and articles, which are classified by code according to a comprehensive outline of human culture. The files also include copies of the original books from which the pages in the files are taken.

Thus, one finds "national character" in the coded *Outline of Cultural Materials* (the code number is 181), and then looks under this code number in the file for the particular country or culture in which he is interested. There he may find various references dealing with national character in one way or another.

Other categories in the *Outline of Cultural Materials* may also be of use in investigating national character. Each has its code number.

The information for the nations and cultures included in these files is not yet complete, nor have files been set up for all modern nations so far. The work is continuing.

HRAF also publishes Area Handbooks, which have included a number of modern nations. In these handbooks, a synthesis of works by members of various disciplines on a particular area is attempted. Several of these which seemed outstanding for their treatment of national character have been included in the present Supplement, but most handbooks have at least a short section on national attitudes, in addition to short general descriptions of the peoples of the area. The coverage is usually too compressed to offer a useful explanation of national character, but the extensive bibliography included in each handbook may furnish leads.

Further information regarding the work of HRAF may be obtained by contacting any of the universities listed above, or by writing directly to: Human Relations Area Files, Box 2054, Yale Station, New Haven, Connecticut.

INDEX

Numbers in parentheses refer to the Bibliography. Page numbers followed by (*q.*) are those on which the entry is quoted. Page numbers followed by (*def.*) are those on which a word or term is defined. References to authors and works in the Supplement appear as follows: Author, Middle East, (*Sup.*) 234; and Middle East, (*Sup.*) 234.

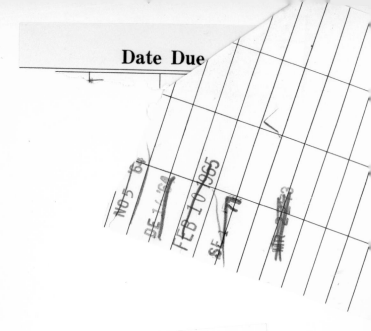

Date